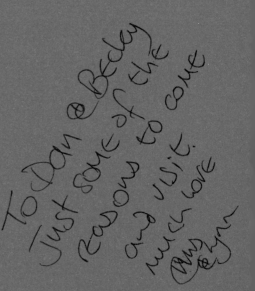

To Dan & Becky
Just some of the
Reasons to come
and visit.
much love
Carolyn

Landmarks of Britain

Landmarks of Britain

Abbeydale Press

First published in 2003 by Abbeydale Press
An imprint of Bookmart Limited
Desford Road, Enderby
Leicester LE19 4AD
England

© 2003 Bookmart Limited

ISBN 1-86147-112-2

Written and edited by Amy Williams
Historical Consultant: Rodney Castleden
Production by Omnipress, Eastbourne

Front cover picture acknowledgement:
Photography by Colin Palmer – www.buyimage.co.uk – contact 01279 757917

Printed in Hong Kong

Contents

Introduction

William Shakespeare once wrote of his homeland, Great Britain, that it is, '...a world by itself'. The description is an accurate one, for Britain is one of the most diverse countries in the world. Geographically, Britain comprises clay valleys, limestone hills and chalk downs. Flat landscapes and low-lying marshlands contrast with isolated mountainous regions. Its rugged coastlines, wild moorlands, deep lakes and enchanting forests have all been beautifully and silently formed over thousands of years.

Historically, Great Britain is equally eclectic. Man migrated to Britain at a time when it was still joined to continental Europe by a land bridge. Settlers came to the moorlands and coastline caves, where they left behind little other than archaeological evidence of their existence. Factual knowledge of this period is extremely limited, and consequently the origins of monuments such as the enigmatic and awe-inspiring stone circle of Stonehenge can only be speculated upon.

The Romans invaded and conquered in 55BC and although these Imperial rulers remained for only four hundred years, their developments, customs and beliefs left an indelible mark on Great Britain. Clear physical evidence remains of their phenomenal defensive fortifications, daily routines, art, culture and palatial life, and the roads they built still form the backbone of Britain today.

In the centuries which followed the fall of the Roman Empire, the invading Angles, Saxons and Jutes fought for supremacy. Anglo-Saxon domination ensued until 1066, when King Harold was defeated by William, Duke of Normandy, at the pivotal Battle of Hastings. The Normans consolidated their hold on England first, and then spread their control throughout the British Isles. Under Norman rule, Great Britain was safeguarded against further attacks, and the implementation began of a number of institutions – religious, political and administrative – of which the essence, and in many cases the actual buildings, still exist today.

A rich array of kings and queens followed William the Conqueror, and during the Middle Ages accession to the throne of England was fiercely contested. When Henry VII took up his crown following the Battle of Bosworth Field, it marked the end of the Wars of the Roses, and the rule of the Tudors began. This was a turning point in the history of Britain for this period saw England emerge as one of the world's leading powers.

Discontent grew in the early seventeenth century, and Civil War resulted in the abolition of the monarchy, which was not resumed until the death of Oliver Cromwell, head of state, in 1660.

During the seventeenth and eighteenth centuries, Britain came to the forefront of European commerce, and during the Industrial Revolution, she established herself as the first industrial power in the world. British power grew, and by the Victorian era, Great Britain was the most powerful country in the world – financially, militarily and territorially.

Great Britain declined during the twentieth century. Her colonial empire fragmented, and although she emerged victorious from the two world wars, she had suffered great losses and had been considerably weakened, economically and demographically. At the dawn of the twenty-first century, Great Britain stands as a powerful force on the world stage, and on the edge of a united Europe in which she must decide whether to take her place or to remain as a separate nation on its outskirts.

The landmarks of Great Britain tell of this illustrious history, but they commemorate not only the kings of queens who have ruled this island nation, but also bear an enduring testament to the genius of architects and engineers, present the humble beginnings of its greatest poets, playwrights and musicians, celebrate the achievements of politicians and statesmen, and pay tribute to the heroic actions of those upon whom the security of the nation has, in times of crisis, depended.

10 Downing Street

Sir Robert Walpole
First Lord of the Treasury,
and the first resident of
No. 10 Downing Street

Number 10 Downing Street, a surprisingly modest looking building in comparison with the residences of many other of the world's leading politicians, is the London office and home of the British Prime Minister, and has been so since the property was presented to Robert Walpole by King George II in 1732.

The first house known on the site was that of Sir Thomas Knight, who arrested Guy Fawkes in 1605. With its proximity to Westminster Abbey and Whitehall Palace, the street was recognised as having a huge potential for development by Sir George Downing, a Harvard graduate, Cromwellian civil servant, and later, faithful subject of the King and Crown. Downing secured leases on the street and its poor quality houses in 1682, and began the work which he was never to see finished. He died two years before the completion of the sturdy looking properties of the street which was subsequently to bear his name.

The houses were inhabited by private residents until the early 1730s when the last resident moved out. In 1732, Count Bothmor, who had been living in a grand property to the rear of Downing Street overlooking St. James's Park and the Horse Guards' Parade, passed away. It was following his death that this residence and the house behind it on Downing Street were presented to Robert Walpole by the King. As a gift, these properties were not accepted, but rather Walpole requested that the houses be made available for his own use, and for the use of all future First Lords of the Treasury, who were later to be more commonly known as Prime Ministers, in an official capacity.

By 1735, when Walpole took up residence, Number 10 (at the time Number 5, but renumbered in 1779) had been linked to the much grander house behind it by the architect William Kent. The main entrance, as we still know it, faced out on to Downing Street.

Downing Street has seen many changes, and of the original row of terraced houses, only four now remain, all addressed consecutively, and all on its north side. Number 9 is the Downing Street entrance to the Privy Council office and now houses the Chief Whip's Office; Number 11 became the official residence of the Second Lord of the Treasury, now Chancellor of the Exchequer, in 1828; and Number 12 contains the Prime Minister's Press Office, Strategic Communications Unit, and Information and Research Unit.

Although they are the 'official residences' of the Prime Minister and the Chancellor of the Exchequer, Numbers 10 and 11 have not always been used in this capacity. By Walpole's successors, Number 10 was used more frequently for official duties than as a residence and it was only with the appointment of Arthur Balfour in 1902 that the tradition of living in the property became firmly established. Throughout the history of these houses, ministers have lived by agreement in whichever rooms they deemed appropriate. During his last period in office, and acting as both Prime Minister and Chancellor of the Exchequer in 1881, Gladstone secured residence in numbers 10, 11 and 12 for himself and his family. In the 1950s and '60s Harold Macmillan lived at Number 10, and reportedly enjoyed having his grandchildren to stay while he continued with official business. Only once has a Prime Minister been forced to leave this accommodation. This occurred in 1940 when, on

Queen Elizabeth II and Prime Minister Tony Blair
outside Downing Street following a reception to celebrate
the Queen's Golden Jubilee

October 14, a bomb landed on Treasury Green, causing extensive damage to the house. As a result, Winston Churchill and his wife moved out of Downing Street and into more secure accommodation in the Number 10 annex above the Central War Rooms. Churchill did however, continue to use the house as an office and did so until the main body of the government was moved into the underground Cabinet War Rooms. In total, 51 Prime Ministers have resided in Downing Street since the property was presented to Walpole.

As a security precaution, steel gates now bar the public entrance to this exclusive street. Although they have been the target of terrorist attacks, the gates are more frequently the scene of small scale demonstrations and protests.

Abbey Road

Although most widely recognised as the location for the majority of the Beatles' recordings between 1962 and 1970, the EMI studios, or 'Abbey Road Studios' as they were renamed in 1969, had already had a long and distinguished history before the Beatles, and now, four decades later, continue to be a hugely successful, busy working studio. In more than 70 years since the doors of EMI opened, recording sessions have been held, and music has been produced, in a wide variety of musical genres.

The building in Abbey Road was originally a large private house, and remained so for almost a century after its construction in 1830. It was in 1927, however, and in view of the rapid growth of the British recording industry, that Ozzy Williams suggested that the building could be successfully employed as a recording studio. Williams was not present for the opening of his dream, as he died before completion of the studios, but in 1931 the doors of The Gramophone Company Ltd, now Electrical and Musical Industries Ltd (EMI), were officially opened. Created primarily for the recording of classical music, the studios were fittingly opened with Sir Edward Elgar's conducting the London Symphony Orchestra's recording of *Land of Hope and Glory*.

Intended for such exclusive classical music recordings, Studio One was built specifically to hold grand orchestras and full choirs. With such features, and with the introduction of recording tape in the 1940s, and LPs in the 1950s, the studio flourished, and in that time produced some of the greatest classical recordings ever made.

Moving with the times, the studio was beginning to embrace pop music by the end of the 1950s, but it was on June 6, 1962 that history was made with the arrival of the Beatles. The group which first arrived at the studio for their audition with George Martin consisted of John, Paul, George and Pete Best. When they returned to Abbey Road to record *Love Me Do*, Pete Best was no longer in the band, and his place had been taken by Ringo Starr.

'If you believe as I do that a house has atmosphere capable of absorbing the personalities and emotions of its inhabitants, you will have no difficulty in appreciating the unique quality of Abbey Road.'
– GEORGE MARTIN

The ensuing popularity of the Beatles affected not only the status of the Abbey Road studios, but also their development and working practices. The Beatles began their recording career as did any other group, maximising the short periods of time which they were able to book in the studios. However as their success grew, and their albums became more intricate, their demand grew for longer studio sessions and the engineers at Abbey Road had to work harder to meet their requirements. Whereas previously the studios had been in control of how and when groups recorded, the Beatles began to involve themselves more in the actual recording process. When the Beatles separated and embarked upon solo careers in the early 1970s, Pink Floyd took their place as the number one band at Abbey Road. Like the Beatles, they did not adhere to the general working practices of the studios and caused huge problems with their lengthy recording sessions. These are now common practice.

Since the 1980s, the demand for classical music had fallen, and therefore the studios turned to big pop and rock bands to utilise the large studios. In addition to this, Abbey Road has also been the location for the recording of many film scores. With its world-renowned acoustics, and ability to accommodate a full symphony orchestra and 120 voice choir, Studio One has attracted producers and film-makers from both Europe and from the bright lights of Hollywood, and is responsible for film soundtracks such as *Star Wars The Phantom Menace*, *Braveheart*, *Harry Potter and the Philosopher's Stone* and *The Lord of the Rings*. The recording and production of film music is now an integral part of the Studios' work.

Perhaps more instantly recognisable than the building or the Studios themselves is the pedestrian crossing located just outside the Studios. Featured on the cover of the 'Abbey Road' album, the crossing is a mecca for Beatles fans, and is now one of London's major tourist attractions.

Aintree Racecourse

Aintree racecourse in Liverpool is the venue for one of the world's most famous and most prestigious horse races, the Grand National. A premier annual event in the racing calendar, it has gone down in the annals of sporting history for its dramatic events, successes, failures and outstanding individual horses. Crowds of 100,000 spectators and television audiences worldwide of approximately 600,000,000 bear witness to the phenomenal global popularity of Aintree's most well known race.

The first Grand National was run on February 26, 1839, and was won by a horse named Lottery, carrying 12 stone. The first official races at Aintree had however, been staged a decade earlier in July 1829. Mr William Lynn, the owner of Liverpool's Waterloo Hotel organised the first flat fixture on the land which he had leased from the Second Earl of Sefton. In 1949, the course was sold by Lord Sefton to the Topham family, a family who were already owners of considerable areas of land around Aintree and who had also been overseeing much of the management of the course since the early years of the Grand National. The further management of the course was then entrusted to Mirabel Topham.

Mrs Topham brought fresh thinking and innovations to Aintree, and saw many new ideas implemented. It was under her management in 1953 that the Mildmay course was opened. This was a new track built within the existing National course, and named after Lord Mildmay, an avid supporter of the Grand National and keen recreational jockey himself. Also under her management in 1953, the motor circuit was opened. Although less of a feature than the world-famous racecourse, the motor circuit was soon reputed to be one of the best in the world and came to host the European Grand Prix and five British Grand Prix.

Red Rum.
Three times a winner, he became the most famous horse in the history of the Grand National

The management and maintenance of the course became increasingly financially difficult during the war and in the years which followed. By 1965 problems had escalated beyond resolution, and plans were initiated to sell the course to a property developer. Thus, every year which followed brought the announcement that it was to be the last Grand National. It was not until 1973 however that the course was actually sold to Bill Davies, a property developer who vowed to continue this much-loved annual event. His resolution was unfortunately half-hearted and when he tripled the admission price for the event in 1975, it saw the lowest attendance in its history, and the future was looking bleak. Ladbrokes, the bookmakers, then entered into a deal with Davies. They agreed to manage the race, which they did successfully for eight years, but Davies was thereafter unwilling to renew their contract. Aintree's future once again appeared uncertain.

This state of affairs generated a huge drive by not only those in the racing spheres, but also within the general public, to save Aintree and the Grand National, and in 1983, with generous donations, The Jockey Club met Davies's asking price and Aintree was sold. Sponsorship came first from *The Sun* newspaper, although this lasted only for the 1983 race. In 1984 *Seagram Distillers* took over sponsorship, which was then passed over to their subsidiary *Martell* in 1992. *Martell* still sponsors the entire event, and over a decade on, Aintree continues to enjoy the successes of this mutually profitable relationship.

The Grand National covers a distance of 7.2 km (4.5 miles) – two complete circuits of the 3.6 km (2.25 mile) course. Over the 3.6km, there are sixteen jumps, all repeated on the second circuit except for the The Chair and The Water Jump, making a total of thirty jumps over the 7.2 km. Of all thirty jumps throughout the course, The Chair and Becher's Brook are the most notoriously difficult, and further the course's reputation as one of the most testing races in the world.

April 2002 – Bindaree jumps the Chair at Aintree's Grand National

Althorp

Althorp has been home to the Spencer family since the beginning of the sixteenth century, and has always enjoyed a prestigious reputation for its beautiful setting and for housing one of the most superb collections of fine art and china throughout Europe. However, this family home was thrust into the spotlight in the late summer of 1997, following the death of Diana, Princess of Wales.

The 300 acre estate around Althorp upon which the house was constructed was acquired by Sir John Spencer in 1508, 20 years after his uncle had become a tenant there; it had become the principal home of the Spencer family by the end of the sixteenth century. The house has undergone many changes and renovations over the centuries, but the shape of the original house can still be seen in the house which currently stands.

It is estimated that the original house remained unaltered until the mid-seventeenth century when some work was carried out by the First Earl of Sunderland's widow. The Second Earl of Sunderland commandeered a more notable overhaul. The changes he made were mostly due to vanity. He was a very well-travelled and fashion-conscious man, and also wished for his residence to reflect his social status.

The first action he took was to employ an Italian architect to transform the exterior of the house, replacing the red-brick walls with a more classical façade. French designers brought Parisian plans for the garden, and upstairs in the house, the west wing underwent work to replace the very Elizabethan great hall with the long gallery. Work was continued by the Fifth Earl of Sunderland circa 1730–32, again for cosmetic purposes.

However, due to poor maintenance by the First Earl of Spencer, whose preoccupation was the construction of Spencer House, his London Mansion, the building began to deteriorate and in 1772 some of the roof collapsed.

This disrepair was not addressed until the succession of his son, who employed the architect Henry Holland (also responsible for some of the work on the Prince Regent's Royal Pavilion in Brighton). Similarly to the Second Earl of Sunderland, the work carried out on the house reflected the financial standing and fashionable requirements of its occupant, but it also reflected the innate Englishness and respect by the architect of the house's Caroline and Palladian background.

Henry Holland used brick-substitute tiles on the walls, affixed gables to the north and south fronts, corridors to the wings, ornamental columns to the front entrance, lowered the roof, moved the state rooms to the west wing, and rebuilt the chimneys. Internally, practicality dictated design, and resulted in less grandeur but more domestic convenience. The then Lady Spencer was full of praise for the design. Compared to Spencer House, in busy central London, Althorp represented a haven of comfort and convenience. Externally, the house still adheres to Holland's design. There are classical European characteristics but simplicity and modesty dominate.

The latest addition to the grounds of Althorp is a converted stable block which now serves as a museum devoted to the life and works of the late Princess of Wales, Lady Diana Spencer. Exhibits include personal items such as childhood letters and her school reports, as well as her bridal gown and details of the work she did for charities. The museum attracts thousands of visitors weekly from all over the world.

Diana herself has been laid to rest in Althorp although her burial place is not accessible to the public. She is buried on an island in The Oval, a beautiful lake within Althorp's Pleasure Garden, and is overlooked by an ancient arboretum which contains trees planted by her sons, William and Harry, the Prince of Wales and other members of the Royal Family.

Diana's memorial at Althorp

Above and below: Althorp House and grounds

Right: Aerial view of the Althorp estate, including The Oval, the island in the middle of the lake on which Diana is laid to rest

Angel of the North

Standing at 20 m (66 ft) high and 54 m (177 ft) wide, the Angel of the North is an imposing, modern-day sculpture located on a panoramic hilltop setting on the approach to Gateshead, at the entrance to Tyneside. Seemingly either loved or loathed, the Angel, and more importantly the £800,000 spent on its construction, is the subject of some very mixed opinions.

The Angel was commissioned by Gateshead Council, funded by the National Lottery through the Arts Council of England, the European Community European Regional Development Fund and Northern Arts, designed by the internationally renowned sculptor Antony Gormley, and made by Hartlepool Street Fabrications. Some believe that the Angel represents rebirth, and is thus a symbolic landmark in an area which has seen massive social and economic changes. Located on a former colliery pit head baths on the boundary of the Great Forest, the Angel also stands as a tribute to the engineering skills of the North East.

The man given the task of creating the Angel, Antony Gormley, is a British artist who was born in 1950, and whose work has been celebrated since its emergence in the 1980s. Winner of the Turner Prize in 1994, and awarded an OBE for his services to sculpture in 1997, he has exhibited his works extensively in the UK and globally. The sculpture was his own response to the area which had already been selected as the site for a landmark work

of art. According to Gormley the function of the Angel is three-fold. The first, he says, is historic. The Angel serves as a reminder that for 200 years coal miners worked in the dark beneath the site. The second represents the progression from the age of industry to information, and the third is as a 'focus for our hopes and fears'.

Gormley initially began work on the Angel by making casts of his own body, and thus it took on the appearance of a human form. The shapely yet genderless contours of the body are sharply contrasted

Work began on the foundations of the Angel in September 1997, and by February 1998, the Angel of the North was on site

with the rigid angles of the wings. The Angel is a warm red colour, an effect achieved by the copper which is present in the special weather-resistant steel of which the sculpture is constructed. The copper oxidises, leaving a thin layer which, over time, turns to a red-brown colour.

At an equivalent height of four double-decker buses, and with an almost equivalent wingspan as that of a jumbo jet, the Angel is a colossal landmark. 100 tonnes of its overall 200 tonne weight is in the main body, and the wings weigh in at 50 tonnes each. Huge concrete piles, with a depth of 20 m (66 ft), have been installed beneath the structure in order to firmly secure it to the unyielding rock below, and enable it to bear winds of more than 160 km.p.h. (100 m.p.h.). It is estimated that the Angel will stand for more than 100 years. Internal maintenance and inspections have been made possible by the inclusion of an access door into the hollow body, located on a shoulder blade.

The Angel's warm red colour is achieved by the oxidisation of the copper present in the steel

Arundel Castle

Arundel Castle, in the beautiful surroundings of West Sussex, overlooking the River Arun and South Downs, was founded by the Earl of Arundel, Roger de Montgomery, almost a millennium ago in 1067. The primary function of the castle, originally constructed as a central motte with two outer walls, was to defend the King's coastline.

The history of the castle is extensive. The Earldom of Arundel was awarded to Roger de Montgomery by King William in recognition of his loyal services and protection of Normandy while the King, then Duke, was fighting at the Battle of Hastings.

Thomas Howard, Fourth Duke of Norfolk

When Roger de Montgomery died in 1094 he was succeeded by his son, Robert de Belleme. However, following his rebellion against Henry I, Belleme was driven out of the castle and the property and lands were seized by the Crown.

The castle remained the property of the Crown until, following the death of her husband Henry I in 1135, Adeliza of Louvain married William de Albini II, and they moved into the castle together. On de Albini's death in 1176, the castle again returned to the Crown, under Henry II. It remained so until, keen to return possession to his family, Richard Coeur de Lion of the de Albinis, made a number of payments to the King in order to secure the castle's return.

Arundel Castle remained with the de Albini family until the death of Hugh de Albini, who died without male descendants, in 1243. It was thus through the marriage of Hugh de Albini's daughter Isobel to John Fitzalan that the castle moved into the Fitzalan family, by whom it was held almost continuously for the following three centuries. In 1555, however, it moved into the Howard family when Mary Fitzalan, last of the Fitzalan line, married Thomas, the Fourth Duke of Norfolk. Here it remains, and is now the residence of the Duke and Duchess of Norfolk and their children.

Such a varied history has had an enormous visible influence on the Castle, and although the Norman origins are still clear, the Castle has undergone much additional construction and adapted the preferred styles of its occupants from over many centuries.

The first centuries of the castle's existence saw the construction of the keep in 1068 and the gatehouse in 1070, and improvements to the domestic facilities, as well as the reinforcement of the castle itself with stronger and more durable stones. The entrance to the keep was reconstructed in the thirteenth century, as was the Well Tower, the barbican and the gateway. The scars of civil war are still present on the gatehouse which was battered during the siege of the castle by General Sir William Waller in the seventeenth century.

Repairs to the castle accelerated from the eighteenth century onwards. Charles Howard, the 'Drunken' Eleventh Duke of Norfolk, a friend of the Prince Regent, designed a complete reconstruction of the castle. This was completed in 1815, and cost the Duke £600,000. The final series of work was begun by the Fourteenth Duke, but following his death, was completed by his son at the turn of the twentieth century, and the Castle as we now see it reflects much of the Fifteenth Duke's work. Retaining its historical appearance, yet moving with the times, the Castle was also among the first country houses to install electric lighting and central heating.

It is not only its constructions and fortifications of which Arundel castle is proud. The Castle boasts an exquisite interior, and houses a fine collection of art, including a specially commissioned portrait of Queen Victoria, and portraits by Van Dyck, Lawrence, Gainsborough and Mytens, as well as clocks, tapestries and furniture dating as far back as the sixteenth century. Many of the treasures within are on display, including personal property of Mary Queen of Scots and pieces from the Duke of Norfolk's collection. In 1846, Queen Victoria visited Arundel for three days. Her dressing rooms, bedroom and furniture were designed specifically for the occasion and are also displayed.

View of Arundel Castle from the River Arun

Balmoral Castle

Situated on the large Balmoral Estate in Aberdeenshire in Scotland, Balmoral Castle was purchased by Prince Albert for Queen Victoria in 1852 and has been a private holiday residence for the Royal Family ever since. The Castle is mainly used by the Queen and her family during the summer months of July and August.

There originally stood a much smaller castle on the Balmoral Estate. This had been built in the fifteenth century, and the first recorded owners were the Abergeldie Gordons. The Castle remained in their possession for two centuries until it passed to the Farquaharson clan in the seventeenth century, and then on to the Earls of Fife in the eighteenth century.

Queen Victoria, following a visit to Scotland, leased the Castle in 1848 for use as a holiday home and declared that, 'It always gives me a pang to leave the Highlands, and this year we have been so especially happy here.'. Consequently, four years later, the Crown purchased the Castle and Estate for the sum of £32,000. However, although the Queen loved the Castle at Balmoral it was considered to be too small for her needs. Prince Albert therefore enlisted the help of William Smith, the City Architect of Aberdeen, and organised the construction of a new building approximately 91 m (100 yards) away from the original. The new Castle was designed in the Scottish Baronial style and made from stone located in the nearby mines of Glen Gelder. It is estimated that the new, enlarged castle could comfortably accommodate 100 guests.

Queen Victoria laid the foundation stone of the new castle in the autumn of 1853, and three years later in 1856 the construction was finished. The old castle was pulled down, and its existence is only commemorated today by a plaque on the front lawn where the front door of the original castle used to stand. On Victoria's death in 1901 the Castle was inherited by King Edward II, and has thus passed down, over time, through his successors.

The Castle, as it is seen today, has remained largely the same since its construction in the mid-nineteenth century. There have however been small additions and amendments made to it by its successive owners. The current monarchy, notably the Queen, and Princes Philip and Charles, closely supervise the running and maintenance of the Castle and Estate. Prince Philip is a particular enthusiast for the gardens of Balmoral, which have been expanded and improved upon by generations of Royals since they were laid out by Prince Albert.

The countryside in which the Estate is located is of a remarkable beauty, and it is believed that it was the woodland near the Castle which particularly drew Prince Albert to Balmoral as it reminded him of Thuringia in his home country. The River Dee runs over 144 km (90 miles) from the Grampian Hills, and offers a series of outstanding views over its course. The nearby Highlands also provide picturesque walks in the attractive countryside. Here stands the Queen's 'Mountain Jewel' and the inspiration for much of Lord Byron's poetry, Mount Lochnagar. It stands at 1,158 m (3,800 ft) high and from its summit the views extend across Scotland. Also in the vicinity of Balmoral is the church of Crathie, the services of which are regularly attended by the Royal Family when in residence, and Abergeldie Castle, 2.4 km (1.5 miles) away, a favourite residence of the Prince of Wales.

The Castle does open to the public, but access is restricted to the Ballroom, and it is only open during the months of April to July when the Royal Family are not in residence. The Ballroom houses an exhibition of Castle memorabilia such as paintings, porcelain and the Royal Tartans and Tweeds. The gardens, planted with rare conifers and trees, are also open, and here can be seen the Garden Cottage which Queen Victoria would often use as a quiet hideaway to manage State correspondence or write her own personal diaries.

The church of Crathie, where the Royal Family attend services whilst in residence at Balmoral

Bath Abbey

In a central location in the city of Bath stands Bath Abbey, one of England's last great medieval churches, which was founded in 1499.

The Abbey is the third church to stand on this site in the city centre. The first church to occupy this position was an Anglo-Saxon Abbey Church. It was constructed in 757, but following the victory of the Norman invaders, in 1066, it was demolished after they seized power. They then began work on a Norman cathedral in 1090. The project however, was too ambitious, and the maintenance of the cathedral was too expensive for the monastery. As a result it fell into disrepair and was in ruins at the end of the fifteenth century.

The Abbey church currently in existence was built in 1499, but suffered under the order of King Henry VIII to dissolve the monasteries in 1539. It was however, salvaged and has undergone many restoration processes to emerge as the Abbey which we see today, still standing over half a millennium since its original construction.

A cleaning and conservation programme, initiated in 2000 has revealed many of the original features of the 1499 construction. Amongst these is the revelation of the outlines and colours of the bath stone which was used in the Abbey's construction.

Much of the Abbey's history, and the history of the city of Bath, is depicted within the Abbey, in its chapels, its stained-glass windows, and on the wall tablets which adorn the Abbey.

The Chapel of St. Alphege commemorates the life of Alphege, once Abbot of the original Anglo-Saxon church, then Bishop of Winchester, and finally Archbishop of Canterbury. As Archbishop he was captured in 1006 by invading Vikings, who issued a ransom for his release. Alphege refused to ask his people

The interior of Bath Abbey

for such an extortionate amount of money, and consequently, after months of imprisonment, he was beaten to death by his captors for his persistent refusals. The Chapel was built in his honour in 1997.

The Edgar Window, at the eastern end of the Abbey also depicts a monumental event in the history of the first church, and also in the history of the British monarchy. It was in the church, in 973, that the coronation took place of Edgar, Prince of the Royal House of Wessex and King of Mercia, and subsequently first ruler of England. As well as the depiction of the coronation on the window, a stone marks the visit of the Queen and the Duke of Edinburgh who came to the Abbey in 1973 to celebrate the thousandth anniversary of England's first coronation, the order of service of which has served as the foundation for all the coronation ceremonies in England since.

Also a recurring feature throughout the Abbey is its coat-of-arms, featuring the keys of St. Peter and the sword of St. Paul. Many other shields adorn the walls and windows.

Before the introduction of street lighting in Bath, the Abbey was known locally as the 'Lantern of the West'. This was due to the installation of 52 windows which cover much of the Abbey's wall space, and through which the light from within the Abbey shone out on to Bath. Most of the glass in the windows is Victorian, although some dates back to the seventeenth century. The windows mainly illustrate stories and characters from the Bible.

Also occupying much of the Abbey's wall space are the hundreds of memorial tablets, created and displayed in recognition of the lives and achievements of many noteworthy and honoured parishioners of the Abbey.

Battle Abbey

Battle Abbey stands on the site of the Battle of Hastings, one of the most famous conflicts in British history, fought between the Norman Duke William and the Saxon King Harold in October 1066. It is believed that the altar of the Abbey Church was placed by William on the very spot where Harold met his death. The motivation for the construction of the Abbey is not entirely clear but it has been recorded that it was a move by William to make amends for the destruction and carnage of the battle. It would serve as both a memorial to those who had lost their lives, and also create a community in a coastal area which was underpopulated and had proved itself to be susceptible to attack. The name Battle Abbey was chosen in commemoration of the battle itself.

On William's orders in 1070, four monks from a Benedictine Abbey in the Loire region of France travelled to England to oversee the construction of the Abbey and to begin the community. By the end of the eleventh century, the building was complete, the church was consecrated, and the monks moved from their temporary accommodation into the stone buildings.

On William's death, the community was flourishing and the Abbey had become incredibly affluent, among the richest in England. The fortunes of the Abbey were further increased with the inheritance of the land which surrounded it for 2.4 km (1.5 miles). This land was cultivated and carefully maintained, and increased its value four-fold over 30 years.

Over the years more land was left to, and often purchased by, the Abbey, increasing its fortunes considerably. The rise in its fortunes however, was in turn creating problems. The Abbey had been set up by William as an establishment which was free from episcopal control, and it had retained this status throughout the reigns of both William I and II. The Bishop of Chichester, in whose diocese Battle Abbey lay, could see the obvious benefits of gaining control of Battle, and the discontent escalated until the Bishop excommunicated the Abbot of Battle. The argument was then taken before the King, and eventually resolved by Henry II and Thomas Becket. They declared that the Abbey was to remain independent from the Bishop, as originally intended by William. Perhaps predictably, this only quietened the bishops temporarily. In the reign of King John, only a substantial payment to the King was adequate to secure the Abbey's status, and when in 1222, the Abbey was again attacked by the Bishop of Chichester, an arrangement was made whereby the Bishop gained certain rights to preach to the monks, on invitation only, and to monitor the election and appointment of new Abbots.

In an excellent financial position due to the shrewd control of its revenue, the Abbey underwent large construction projects in the thirteenth and fourteenth centuries. Reinforcements to the Abbey had been well-timed for French invasions were on the increase, and the Abbey played a crucial role in the protection of the coast and the provision of food and clothes for those who had had to flee their homes. With a slightly depleted revenue due to these attacks, and also as a result of the Black Death, the Abbey again had to take strict control of its finances, and building resumed in the fifteenth century.

The worst chapter in the Abbey's history was yet to come, when in 1538 the Abbot John Hammond was forced to surrender the Abbey to Thomas Cromwell. The estate was then granted to Sir Anthony Browne, who immediately demolished the Abbey church and some of the cloisters, and began the construction of a mansion for himself. When he died, the Abbey remained within his family. The maintenance however was neglected, and over the next two centuries its condition deteriorated. The eighteenth century saw further demolition of the monastic buildings, and improvements and extensions to the mansion. In the nineteenth century a library was built and various renovations made to the parts of the Abbey which had suffered severe damage. After the First World War, Battle Abbey School was established in the mansion and, one of the most acclaimed schools in East Sussex, still remains on the site today.

Beachy Head

At 162 m (531 ft) above sea level, the cliff known as Beachy Head, on the coast of Eastbourne in East Sussex, is the highest chalk sea cliff in Great Britain. The name, mistakenly interpreted as relating to the beach at its foot, is a corruption of the Norman French *Beau Chef*, meaning *Beautiful Headland*. It constitutes a section of the only remaining undeveloped and unmanaged cliffs in Sussex, and marks the eastern end of the range of the South Downs. It is one of the most dramatic landmarks of the south coast.

The cliffs at Beachy Head are magnificent, and the summit is visited by walkers and tourists daily. The rolling hills of the Downs extend to the north and west, and the tide which laps the shore at the base of the cliffs follows the coastline east towards Hastings. To the west, the views stretch past Seaford Head, and on to Brighton.

The cliffs are however as treacherous as they are beautiful, and it is believed that warning lights, in many different forms, have been in place on the cliffs for almost four centuries. At the beginning of the nineteenth century, the precautionary actions taken by the local men were proving so successful that they

The Belle Toute lighthouse

The cliff collapse at Beachy Head

inspired the construction of the Belle Toute lighthouse in 1832. The Belle Toute lighthouse was positioned high up on top of the cliffs at Beachy Head. However, due to its clifftop location, the warning light was often masked by heavy fog and consequently not visible to the approaching ships. It was therefore replaced in 1902 by the current lighthouse which was positioned more suitably 165m (541 ft) out to sea on the shore platform in front of the cliffs. This lighthouse was manned until it became automated in 1983.

The Belle Toute lighthouse is the only lighthouse in private occupation in Britain, and is still standing. Its position however, is precarious. As a result of coastal erosion, the cliffs have begun to fall away into the sea, causing the coastline at Beachy Head to change considerably over the years. The biggest recorded cliff fall in Beachy Head's history occurred in January 1999, when, following a winter of wet weather and storms, a 200 m (218 yards) section of the cliff, weighing thousands of tonnes, crashed on to the beach below and was visible 4.8 km (3 miles) away at sea. Huge chalk boulders rolled over 100 m (109 yards) out across the shore platform.

Coastal erosion is jerky and estimated to take place at an average rate of 0.5–1 m (0.6–3.2 ft) annually. This is a natural process, and explains the spectacularly white appearance of the cliffs, the old chalk having been removed to reveal the new. For this reason, the construction of sea defences to prevent erosion has been forbidden, but with the increase in global warming and the consequent rise in sea levels, this rate of erosion looks set to accelerate, and dramatic cliff falls will become more common.

The cliffs are not only visually fascinating, but they are also of extreme geographical and geological importance, and much of the land has been named as a site of special scientific interest. Archaeologists have found evidence that the area has hosted human activity for thousands of years. Artefacts from neolithic man, bronze age settlements, iron age settlements, and the Romans have been located at this site. Nature enthusiasts are drawn to the area by the plants and insects which are to be found in the many different habitats offered by the cliffs and scrublands, and birdwatchers too, are entertained by the thousands of different species of birds who stop at the headland on their annual migration.

Ben Nevis

Towering 1,343 m (4,406 ft) above the town of Fort William, situated on Loch Linnhe, Ben Nevis is the tallest mountain not only in Scotland, but in all of Britain. It was however, not granted this prestigious status until 1847, the previous belief having been held that Ben Macdhui was the higher of the two peaks by 71 m (232 ft). By international comparisons, its height is relatively modest, but the challenge of reaching its summit is accepted by tens of thousands of walkers and climbers every year.

The origins of the mountain's name are not clear, although approximate translations of the Gaelic version, Beinn Nibheis, can be found in Irish and Gaelic, meaning poisonous or terrible. The numbers of tourists who flock to the mountain every day suggest that the apparent fear which the mountain once generated is no longer present.

Ben Nevis and Fort William from Treslaig

There are a variety of routes to the top of Ben Nevis, and although none are easy, they vary quite widely in difficulty. The route most commonly taken to the summit of Ben Nevis follows the pony track, created as the easiest way to access the summit when the observatory was being constructed in 1883. Beginning at sea level, it is a hard task, but one which requires stamina rather than climbing expertise. Conversely, the north-east face is renowned amongst climbers for the challenge which it poses. The cliffs of the north-east face are imposing, and there are a number of rock-climbing options. These are more easily mastered in the summer than in the winter, when ice forms on the face and rock-climbing becomes ice-climbing.

For those who require a compromise between these two routes, the summit is normally approached from the eastern side of Ben Nevis, having negotiated the rocky paths of Carn Mor Dearg and its Arete, which themselves offer spectacular walks and amazing views. The track is enjoyable but encompasses many narrow ridges and certain sections necessitate moderate climbing. As with the north-east face the difficulty of this route is intensified in winter, and snow makes it all the more hazardous. Fatal injuries have been sustained in such conditions.

While it is estimated that the ascent to the summit would take the average walker between four and five hours, the record held for running up and down Ben Nevis currently stands at 1 hour and 25 minutes. This was achieved during the annual Ben Nevis Race, which takes place on the first Saturday in September. The first official race was run in 1937, but its origins date back to August 1895, when William Swan of Fort William ran the distance in 2 hours and 41 minutes.

On a clear day, the views from the summit are breath-taking. Beyond Glen Nevis, which lies to the south, are the Mamores and the mountains of Glen Coe. Eastwards, the views extend across Carn Mor Dearg to Aonach Mor and Aonach Beag. Statistically however, only one day in every six will herald such clear conditions from the summit, for 300 days out of every year the mountain top is enshrouded in mist. On these days, the only views are those across the plateau of the summit itself. It is host to a number of man-made structures, including an emergency shelter, and the ruins of the 1883 observatory which, for 20 years after its creation, provided reports and data on a continuous hourly basis, but was closed down in 1904 when it was used as a hotel until it subsequently fell into disrepair following the Great War.

The view across Loch Eil towards Ben Nevis

Big Ben

The 96 m (316 ft) tall clock tower which keeps time over the Houses of Parliament is one of Britain's most famous landmarks, and indeed one of the most recognisable clocks in the world. Its chimes have heralded the climax of new years' celebrations all over the country since they were first broadcast to the nation in 1923, and its four faces shine out like a beacon when illuminated against the Westminster horizon.

The name Big Ben is mistakenly applied collectively to the clock, the tower and the bell. In fact, 'Big Ben' was the name given to the original 16 tonne hour bell. The origins of this are not clear, but the general consensus is that it refers to Sir Benjamin Hall, Commissioner of Works, who was involved in the plans for the new clock tower.

When the Palace of Westminster was destroyed by fire in October 1834, a competition was run for new designs for the palace. Charles Barry, an architect, won. One of the most notable features of Barry's design was the inclusion of a clock tower, the dials of which were 9 m (30 ft) in diameter, with the quarter chimes struck on eight bells, and the hours to be struck on a 14 tonne bell. Not being a clockmaker himself, Barry solicited designs and estimates from three renowned clockmakers, Dent, Vuillamy and Whitehurst. Eventually, Edward John Dent was commissioned to construct the clock.

A year after he had won the contract in 1852 however, Dent died, and the continuation of the work was undertaken by his son Frederick. In 1854 the clock mechanism was complete, but the tower itself was not. This proved to be fortunate for, as a result, Dent and his associate Denison laboured further on the mechanism and produced the double three-legged gravity escapement, the feature which is responsible for the acute accuracy of the clock.

Workman abseiling down the Big Ben tower to clean the face of the clock

The hour bell and the four quarter bells were cast by John Warner & Sons in 1856. Again, these were not installed due to the tower not being ready, so the hour bell spent its first year being struck regularly in the New Palace Yard. The bell was two tonnes heavier than Denison's specification, so to compensate, the weight of the striking ball hammer was increased. The bell was not strong enough to support this extra weight and eventually cracked in 1857. Blame was allocated by Denison to Warner & Sons for faulty workmanship, and was returned by them to him for using a hammer which was too heavy. The bell, beyond repair, was melted down and recast by The Whitechapel Bell Foundry, this time weighing 13.5 tonnes. This is the bell which still sounds today.

Following the eventual successful installation of the five bells in 1858, the next problem was that of the clock's hands. The original hands were too heavy to function, and when remade, the replacements were found to be even heavier. The third attempt was successful, and consequently the clock was completed and functional on September 7, 1859.

Within a month the replacement hour bell had suffered the same fate as the original, cracking after being struck by the ball hammer. This sparked a fierce argument between Denison and Whitechapel, and during the two years which it took to resolve the dispute, there was no alternative but to strike the hour on the largest of the four quarter bells. Unable to be replaced a third time, the bell was simply turned so that the hammer, reduced in weight, would strike it in a different place and avoid further damage. The bell was once again operational in 1862.

Over a century passed without problems, and the only alterations made to Big Ben were reflective of technological advancements. The dials had originally been illuminated with gas lighting, which in 1906 was replaced by electricity. Six years later in 1912, electricity was also controlling the winding of the clock, the previous handwinding of which had taken two men five hours to complete.

Disaster struck in 1976 when wear and tear caused a shaft within the chiming apparatus to break, the first effect of which was a marked increase in the speed of the chimes, and then its complete destruction. The repair was an arduous task, and was completed a year later.

Blackpool Tower

The best known symbol of Blackpool is the 158 m (518 ft) high Victorian landmark, Blackpool Tower, on the central promenade. Commenced in 1891, and completed in 1894, the Tower was the project of the Blackpool businessman Sir John Bickerstaffe. Having seen the Eiffel Tower on an earlier visit to Paris in 1889 he returned to Blackpool and created the Blackpool Tower Company. The Tower was based on the Eiffel Tower, and the name originally proposed for it was the Blackpool Eiffel Tower. The design however, was stouter, to withstand the strong winds of the Irish Sea, and half the height of the French original.

The Eiffel Tower, Paris Bickerstaffe's inspiration for the Blackpool Tower

Blackpool is one of Britain's most popular holiday resorts, attracting millions of holidaymakers every year, and the Tower was constructed very shortly after the emergence of the town as a top tourist attraction. It cost £45,000 to build, took two and a half years to complete, and comprised of more than 5,000,000 bricks, and 2,500 tonnes of steel. The admission fee when the Tower first opened was the equivalent of 2.5 pence.

In the century of history which the Tower has already accumulated, it has undergone much renovation and repair. For the first three decades of its existence, the Tower was not maintained correctly, and where it had not been properly painted the structure began to corrode. Demolition was considered, but instead a complete overhaul was undertaken. Between 1921 and 1924 all the steelwork in the Tower was replaced or repaired. Now more precautions are taken, and the maintenance of the Tower is monitored daily by a team of painters and welders.

In spite of all the care taken to preserve the Tower, a devastating fire broke out in the Tower Ballroom in 1956, reportedly caused by a discarded cigarette. The fire was contained to the Ballroom, but had it not been for the concrete foundations, and the firemen who battled against the flames, the metal legs of the Tower may have been damaged and the consequences dire. The repairs cost millions, and took one and a half years, but the Ballroom, immaculate once again, re-opened in 1958.

The Tower now boasts seven levels of hugely varied entertainment: children's adventure playgrounds, an aquarium, tea dances, rides and a lift to the top of the Tower, from where the views extend out across Blackpool, its 'Golden Mile', and out to sea. Also located at the top of the Tower is a post-box, installed by the Post Office in 1949 and employed mainly for its novelty value ever since.

The Tower Circus in the basement auditorium is one of Blackpool Tower's main attractions, and was at one time one of the world's greatest circuses. Again inspired by an attraction which he had seen in Paris, John Bickerstaffe included the creation of a circus within the four legs of the Tower in his plans. He had visited the *Nouveau Cirque* in Paris, and had seen the inspirational aquatic performances which were given there. He therefore envisioned the circus ring which, while water fell from the ceiling and poured in from around the circle, would slowly lower and therefore give the impression that the ring was sinking under the water. 10,000 gallons of water are hidden in tanks below the ring's surface. Every perform-ance at the Tower Circus now ends with this unique and spectacular water finale.

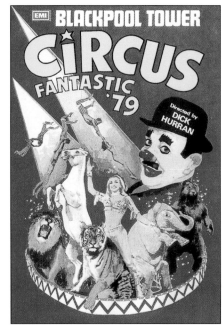

Poster advertising the 'Circus Fantastic' at Blackpool Tower in 1979

From early September until the beginning of November, the 9.6 km (6 miles) of Blackpool's illuminations, stretching down the promenade, are turned on. The equipment used in the staging of the illuminations is worth over £2,000,000, and the production costs over £900,000 annually. The Tower is the star attraction, lit up by over 10,000 bulbs.

Blenheim Palace

In 1704, John Churchill, the First Duke of Marlborough, fought and won what was to become a famous battle on the banks of the river Danube, near the village of Blenheim. He emerged victorious against the army of Louis XIV, and had thus secured safety for the countries of Europe against the invading French forces. For this, and for his numerous military achievements, he was regarded as a national hero. As a reward for his military services, Queen Anne awarded him the Royal Manor of Woodstock and ordered the construction of Blenheim Palace, to be built at her own expense.

The Palace was designed for the Duke and Duchess of Marlborough by Sir John Vanbrugh, and work commenced in 1705. As one of the Queen's obvious favourites however, the Duke was becoming increasingly unpopular among his contemporaries, and over the following years while he was away fighting for his Queen and country, conspiracies were formulated against him. The Queen was influenced and as a result, her gift of money was withdrawn. This left the Duke £45,000 in debt to all those involved in his building project.

Blenheim Palace's Water Garden

All work on Blenheim Palace had stopped by the summer of 1712, and it was only with the death of Queen Anne in 1714 that the Duke approached the builders and suppliers and negotiated the continuation of the Palace's construction. Blenheim Palace was completed in 1722, and in spite of these initial difficulties, it emerged as a magnificent palace in beautiful surroundings, a fine example of English Baroque architecture.

The interior of the Palace is spectacular, and the traits of Vanbrugh's architecture are clearly visible. A typical example of his work can be seen in the Great Hall, where the long corridors extend out from the north and south walls to the wings. The most impressive feature of the Great Hall however, is undoubtedly the 20 m (65 ft) high ceiling, which portrays

Sir Winston Churchill 1874–1965

the Duke's victory at the Danube, and the battle order at Blenheim. This was painted by Sir James Thornhill in 1716.

Since its creation in the first part of the eighteenth century, the Palace has always been the residence of the Dukes of Marlborough of the Spencer-Churchill family. One of the most famous descendants in this line was the grandson of the Seventh Duke of Marlborough, Winston Churchill.

Winston Churchill was born in the early hours of the morning in Blenheim Palace on November 30, 1874, but neither the Palace nor the title which it entailed were ever to be his, passing instead to his cousin, son of the Eighth Duke. Nevertheless, Winston made his love of Blenheim very clear, and of such importance to him that he declared to have chosen it as the place to take '...two very important decisions: to be born and to marry'. He also chose to be buried there in 1965, on the edge of the Blenheim estate, next to his father in the cemetery at Bladon Church.

As well as the paintings of Sir Winston Churchill, British Prime Minister, which hang on the walls of the Palace, an exhibition has also been dedicated to his life and his long and distinguished career. Exhibits include letters, photographs and even locks of his hair which were cut when he was five years old.

Regarded as a site of 'outstanding universal value' by the World Heritage Convention, Blenheim Palace and Park is one of only seventeen World Heritage sites in the UK.

Bosworth Battlefield

The Battle of Bosworth, one of the most significant battles in British history, was fought on August 22, 1485, between Richard III and Henry Tudor. Victory was claimed by Henry, consequently King Henry VII of England, and with it came the end of the Wars of the Roses, and the replacement of the House of Plantagenets with the House of Tudor.

Richard III was born in 1452, the eleventh, and youngest, child of Richard, Duke of York. He grew up under the shadow of the Wars of the Roses, and was eight years old when he was forced to flee with his mother to Burgundy following the death of his father at the Battle of Wakefield. The military victory, and consequent coronation of his brother Edward IV a year later, brought a reversal in Richard's fortunes, and he became the Duke of Gloucester.

Richard's loyalty to his brother and King was unfaltering, and he supported him devoutly in both military battle and in his service. This unerring loyalty had not gone unnoticed, and on Edward's premature death in 1483, he nominated Richard as Protector of the Realm and of his son and heir, who at the time was 12 years old, and not mature enough to assume the position of King for another two years.

The Queen, Elizabeth Woodville, and her relations found this decision absurd, and before Richard had arrived from the north to commence his bequeathed duties, they passed a resolution which replaced Richard's authority with that of a council of regency. As the young Prince Edward began to make his way to London, he was intercepted by Richard who, as his rightful protector, took charge of him and arrested his governor, Earl Rivers. The Queen took her second son and daughters and fled to sanctuary.

Richard then entered London himself and requested the support of his followers in the north to protect him from the Queen, claiming that he feared a continuation of internal feuding if Prince Edward were allowed to become King under the guidance and influence of the Woodville family. Within months he had had the second prince removed from his mother, and sent to join his brother. This was Richard's first step in having the princes disinherited, and those who voiced their opposition to this action were beheaded.

It took just over a month for the old nobility, disturbed by Richard's

Henry Tudor, later Henry VII of England, whose victory over Richard III at the Battle of Bosworth brought an end to the Wars of the Roses

suggestions regarding the implications of a strengthened Woodville family, to declare the succession of Edward V to be illegal. Edward's ineligibility to rule was based on the fact that his father was a bigamist and had already been married when he married Elizabeth. The two princes were therefore both illegitimate, and Richard was the next in line to the throne. Richard received his crown on July 6, 1483.

What happened to the princes in the tower is the most fiercely debated question in British history. That Richard ordered their deaths was never proved, but neither was it disproved. Richard was certainly never able to produce the princes to quash the resentment which was growing towards him as a result of the public belief of his guilt. The theory has also been put forward that Henry VII was responsible for their disappearance and subsequently fuelled the rumours of Richard's involvement in order to discredit him.

Richard's reign was short-lived and not a happy one. A rebellion rose up against him, and although it was swiftly quashed, the strength of feeling was clear. The prospect of an invasion by Henry Tudor was a permanent threat, and when Richard's only son died in 1484, Henry became Richard's rival claimant to the throne of England. Richard was no longer loved by all his subjects, and when Henry Tudor landed in Wales in August 1485, he gathered men, Yorkists and Lancastrians alike, who marched with him to Leicester, and to the field of Bosworth. Henry and Richard's armies faced each other on the morning of August 22 at Ambien Hill, and the last battle of the Wars of the Roses began.

The battle is believed to have taken only two hours. Richard's army was larger, and he was an experienced soldier, but when some of his own men switched allegiance and joined Henry in the midst of battle, Richard and his army were overwhelmed. History records Richard's death as a valiant one, fighting to the very end. It also states that his crown was found hanging on a bush, from where it was taken and placed on Henry VII's head, thus marking the last occasion on which a Crown changed hands on the field of battle.

The battlefield was opened to the public for the first time in 1974 by Leicestershire County Council, who created footpaths across the field and erected information boards to explain the sequence of events as they occurred. The spot where Richard is believed to have fallen is also commemorated with a memorial stone and plaque.

Brecon Beacons

Parc Cenedlaethol Bannau Brycheiniog, Brecon Beacons National Park, was formed in 1957. It is only 24 km (15 miles) from the northern to the southernmost points, and 45 miles from east to west. In that relatively small area the park covers around 1,295km^2 (500 miles^2) and hosts four mountain ranges, including the Brecon Beacons, after which the park was named. The Beacons, in turn, take their name from their previous use as signal beacons.

The Brecon Beacons are the central mountain range, flanked by Fforest Fawr to the west, further behind which lies the solitary Black Mountain, and the repetitively named Black Mountains to the east. The highest point of the Brecon Beacons is Pen-y-Fan, which stands at 886 m (2,907 ft) above sea level, and from which the spectacular views are greatly sought by the hikers who come to the region. This summit and the 3,200 hectares of area which surround it are protected by the National Trust. This includes a natural amphitheatre immediately below the ridges of Pen-y-Fan, which was formed during the Ice Age approximately 10,000 years ago. Pen-y-Fan is the highest point of all the mountains. Waun Fach in the Black Mountains is 810 m (2,660 ft), and Fan Brycheiniog of the Black Mountain stands at 801 m (2,630 ft). The Black Mountain is the least visited of the range, containing wilder and less welcoming walking areas.

The four mountain ranges, surrounded by waterfalls, wooded valleys, lakes and lush hills are magnificently beautiful, and the area offers numerous scenic walking, cycling or pony-trekking paths. Other activities undertaken in the park are canoeing, hang-gliding, fishing, caving and rock-climbing. In the southern area of the park there are a number of limestone caves, some of which are among the longest and deepest in Britain. The River Wye is regarded as the best salmon river outside Scotland, and the River Usk provides brown trout as well as salmon.

The Taff Trail and Offa's Dyke Path are the two main footpaths which traverse the park. The latter 270 km (168 mile) path offers amazing views from the section of the path which crosses through the Black Mountains. The Welsh National Cycle Route, Lôn Las Cymru, passes through the park at 123 km (77 miles) from Cardiff on its way to Anglesey. For boats and barges, the Monmouthshire and Brecon canal, which links Brecon with Pontypool, offers the opportunity to cruise its 53 km (33 mile) course. There are six locks in total over this length, but the longest section without any interruptions stretches for 35 km (22 miles). The canal was originally built at the beginning of the twentieth century for the iron industry, but ceased to be used in the 1930s, remaining inactive until it was restored for the purpose of pleasure boating.

Gerald of Wales wrote of a city submerged in the waters of Llangorse Lake. In 1868, a crannog was discovered, an artificial island, which was an iron age and dark age settlement.

The tranquillity of the Brecon Beacons is reflected in the quiet market town of Brecon, which is the main urban centre located within the park's boundaries. It is a compact town with a population of only 7,000, and is used mainly as a base for visitors who have come to visit the park. It does however have its own history. The fact that the town had been occupied long before the arrival of the Romans in the first century is borne out by the Celtic hill forts of Pen-y-Crug and Slwych. The Romans did not expand the town, which remained the same until the defeat of the local Welsh chieftain by the invading Norman lord, Bernard de Neufmarche, in the eleventh century. Under the new Norman rule a castle was built and a Priory was established on the site of an existing church.

Once a year, in contrast to the serenity of its surroundings, the town hosts the Brecon Jazz Festival, one long party for the thousands of people who descend upon Brecon. It has been heralded as one of the leading Jazz festivals in Europe.

Monmouth and Brecon canal, near Llangattock, Powys

Buckingham Palace

Buckingham Palace is the nucleus of the British monarchy's activities. It is globally recognised as the official residence of the Queen and the Duke of Edinburgh, but it is also the administrative heart of the monarchy. It contains the offices of those who co-ordinate the daily duties and activities of the royal family, as well as providing the venue for official ceremonies and state visits. Buckingham Palace receives an estimated 50,000 guests per year, invited to many different functions including garden parties, banquets and receptions. Certain areas of the Palace are open to the public, and have been so since 1993, but mostly visitors to London and members of the British public alike congregate outside the gates of the Palace to marvel at the splendour of the Queen's home and to see whether she is in residence, as indicated by the flying of the Royal Standard from the roof at the East Front.

Buckingham Palace takes its name from the Duke of Buckingham, who commissioned the building of a townhouse in 1702 to serve as his London home. The House was sold to the Crown in 1762 when King George III purchased it from the Duke's son, and despite the official royal residence being St. James's Palace, King George and Queen Charlotte chose to reside in Buckingham House.

When the throne, and consequently Buckingham House, passed to King George IV on his accession in 1820, he commissioned John Nash, his architect, to transform the existing building into a state palace. He commenced this work by adding wings to the front, and extending the rear of the Palace. This effectively doubled the size of the building. Despite having contributed so much to the creation of the Palace, George IV was never to reside in it for he died before the work was completed. No further work was implemented by his brother and successor, William IV, who also never resided within the Palace walls. John Nash was removed from the project, and the plans for the Palace lay dormant until the reign of Queen Victoria.

The young Queen Victoria had only been reigning monarch of England for three weeks before making the Palace her official home in 1837, a status which it has enjoyed ever since. The only complaint was that the Palace was too small. Ten years later therefore, in 1847, Edward Blore constructed the East Front. The wings built by John Nash were joined, and the forecourt was closed in. The grand garden gateway, now known as Marble Arch, was too narrow for the coaches of George IV and was therefore removed and taken to Tyburn, where it still remains. With the exception of the restyling of the façade in 1912, the Palace has not undergone any changes since.

The Royal Mews is located behind the Palace in Buckingham Palace Road. It was originally home to the royal falcons, but now houses all the state vehicles which are immaculately kept for use on ceremonial occasions. The collection includes the Gold State Coach of 1871, used at the coronation of George IV, and employed at every coronation since, and also the Glass Bridal Coach of 1910, which is used on the occasion of royal weddings. The stables which can be seen in the Mews are those which were rebuilt by John Nash in 1820 after the Mews had moved to the Palace in the 1760s.

Household troops have guarded the monarch and the royal residence since 1660, and in the forecourt of the Palace, this tradition is continued with the Changing of the Guard which takes place daily during the summer months and on alternate days during the winter months. It is a ceremony during which the sentries are changed, and the old guard is relieved of his duties by the new guard.

Buckingham Palace contains one of the most priceless collections of art in the world today, but it is neither a gallery nor a museum. Some pieces from the Royal Collection can, however, be viewed on entry into the State Rooms of the Palace, which is granted to visitors during the annual summer opening. Works on display include paintings, sculptures, tapestries, furniture and porcelain. The State Rooms are used for court ceremonies, and look out on to sections of the 40 acres of private gardens which lie behind the Palace.

The ceremony of the Changing of the Guard, conducted in the forecourt of Buckingham Palace

Burns Cottage

Scottish bard and national hero, Robert Burns is considered by Scots past and present to be one of the most influential figures in Scottish history and, through his work, an ambassador and custodian of the Scottish language, identity and culture. At a time when the unique spirit and character of Scotland were in danger of being swallowed by a common British culture, his writing reawakened the Scottish national identity and left an ineradicable mark on British literature.

Robert Burns, surrounded by his creations

Robert Burns was born on January 25, 1759, near Ayr in Scotland. His father, William Burns, was a poor man yet one who sought a good education for his children. He sent Robert to school in a neighbouring village for three years and greatly encouraged his academic progress. As a result of his father's enthusiasm for education and his own passion for reading, Robert developed a keen knowledge of English and familiarised himself with literary works from Shakespeare to the then contemporary writers.

As a personal interest only, Robert Burns began to write poetry, and it was only as a result of finding himself in circumstances which necessitated the acquisition of enough money to emigrate that he decided to collate them in a volume and put them forward to be published. On the strength of the unexpected success which this volume (*Poems – Chiefly in the Scottish Dialect – Kilmarnock Edition*) achieved, Burns's plans changed and he made his way to Edinburgh where he was greeted by artists, writers and poets, who bestowed an almost celebrity status upon the 'Ploughman Poet'. A larger volume of his poems was produced, but on the money which it brought him, he returned to renovate his late father's farm, where he worked for three years. When this venture failed, he moved to Dumfries and commenced employment in the Excise service to maintain an income. The work was exhausting and demoralising, and throughout this time, he continued to write both poetry and song, producing some of his most famous works such as *Tam O'Shanter*, *The Lea Rig* and *A Red Red Rose*.

Robert Burns died at the age of 37 from heart disease, and more than 10,000 people attended his burial, a mere fraction of the following which he posthumously attracts.

Burns's birthplace, a humble cottage, is now the heart of Burns National Heritage Park in the beautifully scenic Alloway. It is considered to be the most important of the tributes to Burns, and contains many of his early possessions as well as an almost complete collection of his works.

⋆⇒◎⇐⋆

'In this cottage, of which I myself was at times an inhabitant, I really believe there dwelt a larger portion of content than in any Palace in Europe.'
JOHN MURDOCH, Schoolmaster

⋆⇒◎⇐⋆

Burns described his birthplace as the 'Auld Cleg Biggin'. It was erected by his father following the purchase of seven and a half acres of land from Dr Alexander Campbell in 1756. Burns only lived in the cottage until the age of seven, and then moved with his family to Mount Oliphant in 1766. The cottage was subsequently rented out by William Burns until he sold it and its grounds to the Incorporation of Shoemakers for £160. They in turn let the cottage and the land, and by 1800 one of the tenants had converted the property into an ale house. It remained thus until 1881 when, realising the historic importance of the building, the Alloway Burns Monument Trustees took over the property and tore down the constructions which had been added by the Incorporation of Shoemakers, thus revealing the cottage in its almost original state.

Subsequent restoration has been done to recreate the atmosphere of the cottage as it would have been in the eighteenth century, and it is now brought to life through a combination of artefacts from Burns's past as well as a modern audio-visual display.

January 25 has become an annual celebration of the life and works of the Scottish bard. From formal gatherings of erudite scholars to those who celebrate in drunken uproar – the option much preferred by Burns himself – parties are held in his honour all over Scotland.

Caerphilly Castle

A stained glass depiction of Gilbert de Clare

Caerphilly Castle is the largest castle in Wales and, after Windsor, the second largest castle in Britain. Its size, and the military planning upon which its construction was based, places it amongst the greatest medieval castles in all of western Europe. With one of the finest examples of medieval architecture, its concentric arrangement and the virtually insuperable water defences, modelled on those at Kenilworth, the castle was almost completely impenetrable.

The castle was built by Gilbert de Clare, the Anglo-Norman lord of Glamorgan, in the thirteenth century. De Clare was one of Henry III's barons, and was a strong and powerful man. He had captured the region of Senghenydd from the Welsh in 1266 with the intention of halting the southward movement of the Welsh leader, and last native prince of Wales, Llywelyn ap Gruffydd, under whose control already lay the majority of central and north Wales. He constructed the castle at Caerphilly, in Senghenydd, as well as other castles on the northern border which lay between his territory and that of Llywelyn, in order to defend his region. Two years after the building had commenced in 1268, the castle was attacked by Llywelyn. The attack was unsuccessful, and acknowledging his defeat, Llywelyn retreated north, and work continued in 1271.

In order to create the first line of defence, the huge moat, de Clare flooded a valley in which he had crafted three artificial islands. On these islands he positioned his castle. The nucleus of the castle was set on the central island, with the eastern island as a fortified dam, and the western island as a walled redoubt. The section of the castle on the central island was built to serve as a complete castle, independent, if necessary, of the defences to its east and west. As such, further lines of defence were constructed, these being an inner moat and gatehouses. The inner ward was bordered by four curtain walls with four huge, cylindrical towers on each corner, and more gatehouses, each of which could serve as independent castles, able to be closed off and offer complete protection and refuge in the event of the siege of any other areas of the castle.

Henry III died in 1272, and was succeeded by Edward I, a dynamic and outstanding King. In 1277, Edward focused his attention on the situation in Wales, and the unchecked power, and resistance to the English, of Llywelyn. As Edward's armies advanced, Llywelyn's support faded, and he was driven out of his strongholds. The Welsh were subdued and Llywelyn, now only Prince of Gwynedd, was forced to live under English rule. The Welsh were to tolerate this situation for only five years, and rose in revolt in 1282. Llywelyn joined with his brother David and the princes of the south, but the powerful forces of Edward I descended once again upon Wales and crushed the rebellion, executing its leaders. All resistance ceased, and Welsh independence was lost forever.

With Welsh revolt no longer a threat, the need for Caerphilly to serve as a border fortress ceased, and it was mainly used as an administrative centre for the estates of the de Clare family. Henceforth Caerphilly Castle remained relatively inactive, and with the exception of two small-scale attacks in 1294 and 1316, the castle only encountered one major assault. This was between December 1326 and March 1327 when Queen Isabella, mistakenly believing that Edward II was still seeking refuge within the castle's walls, besieged the castle. Edward however, had long been gone by the time she arrived and therefore the siege was to no avail.

Apart from some domestic work and the refashioning of the Great Hall by Hugh le Despenser in the 1320s, the castle remained structurally unaltered, but it did, over the centuries fall into ruin. This was accelerated in the sixteenth century by the permission given to Thomas Lewis of the Van to use stone from the castle to build his house. By the time of the Civil War the castle was in such disrepair that it could not be used, and an earthwork redoubt was built instead.

It was only in the mid-twentieth century that restoration work was initiated, and the lakes, which had been dry for two centuries, were reflooded. The great bulk of the castle has been restored and remains today, and its miraculous engineering is still clear. The effect of the Civil War and attempts to demolish it however, can also be seen on the castle, particularly on the south-east tower of the inner ward, which surviving the gunpowder exploded around it, now leans visibly and seemingly precariously, and is even claimed by some to 'outlean' the Leaning Tower of Pisa.

Canterbury Cathedral

In 597, a missionary sent to England from Rome by Pope Gregory the Great landed on the shore at Kent. He was St. Augustine, and he was to become the first Archbishop of Canterbury. It is believed that Pope Gregory had seen a group of Anglian slaves on sale in the market and, impressed by their beauty, sent Augustine and a group of monks to England to convert the Anglian people to Christianity.

An existing church, which had already been used during the Roman occupation of Britain, was given to Augustine on his arrival by Ethelbert, the local king, whose queen had already converted to Christianity. St. Martin's church stood in Canterbury, and it was here where Augustine, already a bishop, confirmed his seat as the first Archbishop of Canterbury.

Canterbury Cathedral, begun in 602, is composed of a number of architectural styles, developing and changing, as did many great cathedrals, over decades and centuries. St. Augustine's original cathedral was destroyed by fire in 1067, and this presented Lanfranc, the first Norman Archbishop, with the opportunity to re-design a new cathedral. He greeted this with zealous enthusiasm, and the cathedral was built up in a beautiful Romanesque style, with a new impressive nave, and a complete reorganisation of the attached monastery.

Lanfranc was succeeded by Anselm, arguably the greatest of Canterbury's Archbishops, certainly an erudite scholar, and much of the Norman stonework which can be seen today was his inspiration, notably the magnificent crypt beneath the choir.

One of the most tragic, and most landmark events in the Cathedral's history was the slaughter of Thomas Becket, then Archbishop of Canterbury, in December 1170. Although close friends, Henry II and Becket had argued fiercely over the legal control of the clergy. In anger, and in the presence of four of his knights, Henry reportedly cried, 'Who will rid me of this turbulent priest!'. Seizing their opportunity to win favour with the king, his knights despatched immediately to Canterbury and murdered Becket in the north transept, thus martyring him, and henceforth transforming the Cathedral into a

St. Thomas Becket 1118–1170
Murdered by four of Henry's knights
in the cathedral

site of pilgrimage. Abhorred by the consequence of his words, Henry came to the Cathedral the following year, and was whipped by the monks as punishment for his order. Whether this was a political act or genuine atonement has been much debated.

Only four years later, in 1174, disaster struck again when another fire ravaged the eastern half of the Cathedral. With a high income generated by the pilgrimages made to the Cathedral, the monks saw the opportunity to create from the ashes a building befitting the Cathedral's newly acquired status as England's most important centre of pilgrimage.

The French architect, William de Sens, was commissioned and he created the early Gothic style which was to become a feature of cathedrals during this period throughout England. The work de Sens began was continued by William the Englishman, and the grand choir which he completed came to accommodate St. Thomas Becket's shrine. The saint's remains were moved from their original place of burial in the crypt to the choir in 1220, in a magnificent ceremony, attended by such dignitaries as Henry III.

No further work was undertaken on the Cathedral until the end of fourteenth century when construction began on the western half of the building. The new perpendicular style was used to create a new nave where the old Norman one had once stood. Work continued for over a century, concluding in 1500 with the completion of the beautifully decorative fan vault of Bell Harry.

The elite and prestigious status which had been bestowed upon Canterbury Cathedral following the murder of St. Thomas Becket, was, in turn, to be responsible for another tragedy. The wealth generated by the pilgrimages made to the Cathedral heralded its supremacy over all others, and this affluence and power did not escape the attention of Henry VIII and Thomas Cromwell. During the period of the dissolutions the shrine was destroyed, wealth was plundered, and windows and monuments were vandalised. The damage and theft was extensive. Only with the restoration of the monarchy in 1660, and the re-establishment of the Church of England, did life return to the Cathedral, repairs were initiated and daily services were resumed.

Cavern Club

Named after the Parisienne Jazz Club, *Le Caveau*, the Cavern Club, originally a Victorian warehouse, was opened in January 1957. The intention of its owner, Alan Sytner, was to emulate the success of its French namesake, and to establish the club as one of Britain's leading jazz venues.

The club did enjoy success, and attracted both popular artists and jazz devotees, but the jazz craze was soon to be overtaken by the introduction of skiffle. Skiffle music was a brief trend, but one which was to open the music scene up to many of the country's budding musicians. Such was the simplicity of its style that more people experimented with skiffle, and the increase in artists with a desire to perform led to an increase in demand for stages on which to do so.

To meet this demand, the Cavern Club first opened its doors for lunchtime performances in April 1957. In August of the same year The Quarrymen Skiffle Group gave their first performance at The Cavern – one of the band members was the then relatively unknown John Lennon.

These lunchtime sessions were proving to be increasingly popular, and by 1960, jazz had been allocated to the weekend slot. It was eventually taken off the club's line-up completely in 1963. What replaced it were the Beat group sessions, the first of which had occurred in 1960 with a performance by Rory Storm and the Hurricanes, with Ringo Starr on the drums.

The Cavern Club is an independently successful and world-famous club, but it is perhaps for its association with the Beatles that it is most instantly recognised. The Beatles first performed at the Cavern in February 1961, and very quickly began to draw in large crowds. They had just returned from Hamburg where they had been performing for long hours on a nightly basis, and where they had thus developed their unique style.

The Beatles on stage at the Cavern Club

John Lennon's statue outside The Cavern Club

The Beatles dominated the Cavern's stage, and thrust the club into the limelight. It was here that they were approached by Brian Epstein, who offered his services as their manager, and through whom they obtained their first recording contract. In spite of their soaring national popularity however, the Beatles remained extremely loyal to the Cavern and to their fans there, and continued their performances. It is estimated that they performed over 300 gigs at the club between 1961 and 1963.

Such was the phenomenal success of the Beatles that they were soon becoming too big for the Cavern. Pete Best was replaced by Ringo Starr in 1962, much to the initial disappointment of the fans, and their last performance at the club followed shortly after in 1963. In the wake of the Beatles however, Liverpool and the Cavern Club had become a flourishing music scene, and already established celebrities aspired to perform on the Cavern's stage.

Unfortunately, this was not set to continue and the Cavern suffered a reversal of fortunes in 1964. The popularity of Mersey Beat decreased, and ventures into recording failed financially. The final drain on the club's resources was the need to renovate the premises in order to comply with Health and Safety regulations. The club was forced to close in 1966.

Four months later, following huge financial donations, and petitions to the Prime Minister, the Cavern Club was re-opened by Harold Wilson, surrounded by celebrities, and with the best wishes of the Beatles and Brian Epstein bestowed upon it and sent via telegrams. The re-opening was a success, but although the Cavern was financially secure, it never regained its earlier status. The club closed again in 1973, whereupon a new Cavern Club was opened across the road. The club's regulars however, did not move with it.

When John Lennon was assassinated in 1980, the architect David Backhouse proposed to re-open the original underground Cavern as a homage to the world-famous musician. His plans were approved, but on investigation the site was judged unsafe, and it had to be completely demolished. The bricks from the original club were salvaged, and used to re-construct the Cavern on 75 percent of its original site. This was completed and re-opened in 1984. There are now no remains of the original basement cellar club.

Cenotaph

In the middle of Whitehall, the Cenotaph, its name taken from the Greek, simply meaning 'empty tomb', stands as a poignant memorial to 'The Glorious Dead', all those who have given their lives in defence of the freedom of others, many of whom fell in foreign fields and have no tomb of their own.

The Queen lays a wreath, leading the commemorations at the Cenotaph on Remembrance Sunday

Designed by Edwin Lutyens in 1919 in wood and plaster, the Cenotaph was originally intended to be only a temporary structure, erected for the forthcoming Peace Day celebrations of July 19. On hearing that the French, who were celebrating the end of the war with a similar day of commemoration, had erected a huge catafalque for the Allied troops to march past, Lloyd George decided that the British people should have a similar memorial to salute in honour of the dead.

The reason for the proposal of a cenotaph in place of a catafalque was the absence of any religious association. A catafalque was a traditionally Catholic structure, and it was felt that the London memorial should commemorate men and women of all denominations. The Cenotaph which stands today bears no religious symbol, and flies only the flags of the three forces and the Merchant Navy.

The Cenotaph was built in two weeks, and unveiled on the morning of July 19. Wreaths were laid at its base, and the Victory March of fifteen thousand Allied soldiers and leaders, including Haig, Foch and Pershing, saluted it in silence as they passed.

Lutyens's structure, and its symbolism, received phenomenal praise in the days following its unveiling, and the suggestion was soon made that it should be made into a permanent memorial. Agreement was unanimous, with the only debate being whether the positioning of the Cenotaph in six lanes of heavy traffic was suitable. Overall however, it was decided that the Cenotaph had already made its mark on London and that neither the memorial nor the memories of Peace Day should be removed from the original site in Whitehall. The following year, the Cenotaph, constructed of Portland stone, was unveiled and this is the memorial which still stands today.

The tradition of Remembrance Day began, and the Cenotaph immediately became an obvious focus for all those wishing to pay their respects to the war dead of the United Kingdom, the Commonwealth and the British territories. On the Sunday nearest to November 11, the day that the guns had fallen silent in the Great War in 1918, services were held annually throughout the country. With the conclusion of the Second World War in 1945, the services opened up to embrace the memories of the fallen heroes of this second conflict. In 1980 the services were extended further to commemorate all those who had died serving their country in battle.

The service which is held at the Cenotaph is the focus for the nation, and is attended by the Queen, the Royal Family, politicians, representatives from the Armed Forces, and High Commissioners from the Commonwealth countries. Hymns are sung, prayers are said, wreaths of poppies are laid on the Cenotaph's steps, and a two minute silence is observed nationwide. The march past of ex-servicemen and women and civilian organisations then follows the service and lasts approximately one hour. The poppy, the symbol of remembrance, is made and sold in the months prior to Remembrance Day to raise money to help ex-servicemen and their dependents.

⊹⊱⊰⊹

'If ye break faith with us who die, we shall not sleep, though poppies grow in Flanders fields.'
– JOHN McCRAE, May 1915

⊹⊱⊰⊹

Cerne Abbas Giant

There is no conclusive explanation for the existence of the Cerne Abbas Giant, a huge, imposing and mysterious chalk-cut figure carved on to the side of a hill in the village of Cerne Abbas in Dorset. Theories and speculation however, abound.

The outline of the Giant is formed by a trench 0.4 m (1.3 ft) wide, cut into the chalk bedrock beneath. His (for he is undeniably male) height is 55 m (180 ft), and he has a width of 51 m (167 ft). The massive club which he brandishes in his right hand is 36.5 m (119 ft) long.

The earliest reference to the Giant has been found in the account books of the churchwarden of Cerne Abbas in 1694, wherein it is stated that a payment of 3 shillings was made 'for repaireing of ye Giant'. The next written reference to the Giant does not appear again until 1742 when Francis Wise commented that 'it may be of some antiquity'. In 1764, the figure was surveyed and its dimensions were recorded in the *Gentleman's Magazine*. The measurements noted in the magazine confirm that, unlike many of Britain's hill figures, the Giant's shape and size have not changed to any noticeable degree. The only difference between the depiction of the Giant in this account and the figure we see now is in the navel, present in the 1764 publication, but no longer visible, and the shorter penis.

Although references date back only to the seventeenth century, a much earlier origin is suggested by its design, and by its proximity to an Iron Age earthwork.

The once generally supported belief that the Giant was carved in the image of the god Hercules at the end of the second century is now discredited. Hercules is commonly depicted holding a club and skin, and although the skin is not present in any of the early drawings of the Giant, research suggests that he may once have held an object, no longer visible, in his left hand. Geographical surveys show that a cloak was wrapped around the left arm, showing a standard 'cloak shield' for an iron age warrior. These warriors often fought naked, wearing only a belt to hold a dagger. The Cerne Giant still has a belt. Close-contour surveys show that a severed head swung from the left fist, and this too is characteristic of iron age practice. Thus there is mounting evidence that the image shows an iron age warrior, returning victorious from battle. He was perhaps the guardian god of the local tribe, the Durotriges.

Local legend offers numerous explanations for the existence of the Giant. The figure is believed by some to be the outline of a real Danish giant who, having laid down to sleep on the side of the hill, was attacked and decapitated by the Cerne Abbas villagers who then drew around his body to mark the spot where he had met his fate.

Another story credits the monks from the nearby abbey with the creation of the Giant. It is believed that they did this to mock their Abbot, Thomas Corton, who was banished from the monastery for misconduct.

Regardless of the Giant's origins, it has certainly formed the basis of many local traditions and rituals. The most regular tradition associated with the Giant is the May Day celebration, the site of which was actually the small banked earth enclosure, known as The Frying Pan, or Trendle, situated just above and to the right of the Giant's head.

Due to his evident virility, the site of the Giant, and more specifically his penis, was commonly used as an area to make love by couples wishing to conceive. Unmarried women would sleep on the Giant to beget betrothal, and young women were known to walk around the perimeter of the Giant three times in order to keep their husbands or lovers faithful. The original reason for the display of virility was probably quite different; it was just an iron age symbol of good luck.

An aerial view of the Cerne Abbas Giant

Chichester Cathedral

Although a cathedral already existed approximately 16 km (10 miles) away from Chichester in an area near Selsey, and had done for almost four centuries, construction began on a second cathedral in Chichester in the eleventh century. This was in response to the policy introduced by the Norman invaders of basing their sees in the more populated and administrative areas.

Chichester was founded as a see when Selsey Cathedral was destroyed by coastal erosion and Bishop Stigand, Selsey's former Bishop, moved to the old Roman town in 1075, and work commenced on the cathedral in the following year. Construction continued into the next century and in 1108 the building was completed and dedicated to the worship of God.

The original building was to last only six years before damage caused by a fire necessitated restoration work to the Cathedral. This was completed and the building was also extended further westwards. Another fire in 1187 damaged much of the east end of the Cathedral and completely devastated the wooden roof. This set in motion a huge restoration programme and restyling of many of the Cathedral's features. The work was completed by the end of the twelfth century, and the Cathedral was re-dedicated in 1199.

Following the canonisation of Bishop Richard of Wych in 1276 by Pope Urban IV, the Cathedral became celebrated as a place of pilgrimage. His body was moved from where it lay in the Chapel of St. Thomas and St. Edmund, and a shrine befitting a Saint was erected in the Retro-choir, to which pilgrims flocked in their thousands. This shrine suffered the same fate as many other sites of pilgrimage under the reign of Henry VIII and was totally demolished, but an altar still stands to commemorate the life and work of Saint Richard.

'Side by side, their faces blurred,
The earl and countess lie in stone,
Their proper habits vaguely shown
As jointed armour, stiffened pleat,
And that faint hint of the absurd-
The little dogs under their feet.'
— PHILIP LARKIN, *AN ARUNDEL TOMB*

The effigies of Richard Fitzalan III, Thirteenth Earl of Arundel, and his second wife Eleanor, the inspiration for Larkin's 'Arundel Tomb'

The fourteenth and fifteenth centuries witnessed much of the construction of new features and the improvement of existing buildings. The beginning of the sixteenth century saw an overhaul in the administration of the Cathedral, with Bishop Robert Sherburne allocating the responsibility for many of the daily duties to the choir and clergy. The cathedral suffered immense damage during the Reformation, and thereafter it entered a period of neglect which lasted almost two centuries.

Renovations and repairs were eventually initiated in the 1840s by Dean George Chandler, and completed by his successor Dean Walter Farquhar Hook. The only major setback to the work overseen by Hook was in 1861 when the spire of the Cathedral collapsed.

The good structural condition of the Cathedral is maintained by donations from the association of Friends of the Cathedral. Although there are still important renovations to be implemented, recent work has included careful cleaning of the interior stonework, and the restoration of the ceilings.

Inside, the Cathedral houses an impressive collection of treasures, including early carvings, sculptures, paintings and stained glass, some of which depict stories or historical events, such as the Chichester Reliefs which portray the raising of Lazarus. Parts of a Roman mosaic are still visible in the aisle of the south choir. The table tomb of the Thirteenth Earl of Arundel, and his second wife Eleanor dates to the fourteenth century and depicts the couple holding hands. It was the inspiration for Philip Larkin's poem *An Arundel Tomb*. Another impressive feature of the Cathedral is its spire. When the original spire, rebuilt by Sir Christopher Wren in the seventeenth century, collapsed in the nineteenth century it was restored by Sir George Gilbert Scott, and it is this spire which is still in place today.

Clifton Suspension Bridge

*Isambard Kingdom Brunel
1806–1859*

The Clifton Suspension Bridge, which spans the Avon Gorge for a distance of 214 m (702 ft), is one of Bristol's most famous landmarks. Originally proposed to carry only horse-drawn traffic, pedestrians and animals, over 4,000,000 cars now cross the bridge annually, and it can hold vehicles of up to four tonnes in weight.

The origins of the bridge are enigmatic. On his death in 1754, William Vick, an affluent wine merchant, left instructions for the sum of £1,000 to be invested until its value had multiplied ten-fold. This £10,000, he requested, was to be spent on the construction of a stone bridge across the Avon Gorge.

There is no clear reason for this bequest, but in 1793, while the money was gaining the necessary interest, plans were drawn up by William Bridges for the bridge. These however, were extravagant. The designed structure was massive and contained all the amenities of a town–houses, an inn, stables, a library, and many other buildings. As spectacular as this bridge was, the cost was unaffordable.

The accessibility and more frequent use of iron in the early nineteenth century meant that more bridges across Britain were being constructed in wrought iron. Examples include the Menai Suspension Bridge, constructed by the renowned civil engineer Thomas Telford in 1819. Another advantage of iron was the relatively low cost in comparison with stone. To build the stone bridge which Vick had instructed would have cost £90,000. By 1829, his legacy had reached only £8,000.

Therefore in October 1829, a committee charged with the management and administration of the bridge launched a competition, offering a prize of £105, for the best design for the new iron bridge, to be judged by Thomas Telford. On receipt of all the entries however, Telford immediately rejected them all, and instead offered his own design. In turn, when this was shown to the population of Bristol, they dismissed it as ridiculous. Rather than express the views of the town, the committee told Telford that they could not fund his plans, and another competition was subsequently run.

Isambard Kingdom Brunel, who had previously been working on the Thames Tunnel, and who had tendered a total of four entries in the first competition, re-submitted four more designs. On the news that he had come second in the competition, Brunel approached the judges and arranged a meeting in which he managed to convince them that the objections which they had expressed regarding some of the technical aspects of his design were unfounded. Two days later the original competition results were withdrawn and Brunel was declared the winner and consequently project engineer for the bridge. His preferred 'Egyptian' design was the one eventually chosen by the judges.

Despite being £20,000 short of funding, work commenced on the bridge in 1831. This was followed swiftly by the outbreak of the Bristol Riots, which were eventually dispersed by cavalry, but which had done enough damage to destroy business confidence, and therefore delay the continuation of work on the bridge for another four years.

With only the two towers completed and an iron bar stretching across the Gorge, funds ran out in 1843. Amendments were made to reduce the cost, but when Parliament's deadline for completion of the work expired ten years later, there was no choice but to sell off all the iron and machinery to pay suppliers and contractors. Brunel died prematurely in 1859.

Brunel declared the bridge to be his 'first love', his 'darling'

From Brunel's death however, his bridge was to rise, for it was decided by the Institution of Civil Engineers that the most fitting memorial to the great man would be the completion of this project. Money was raised and the task of completing the bridge was given to the engineers Sir John Hawkshaw and W. H. Barlow in a revised Act of Parliament.

The Clifton Suspension Bridge was ceremonially opened on December 8, 1864, 110 years after the death of the man whose vision it had been.

Cutty Sark

The *Cutty Sark*, now restored to her former glory in the permanent dry-dock of Greenwich, was launched as a tea clipper in November 1869 at Dumbarton on the Scottish Clyde. Consistent with her Scottish origins, the ship was named after the 'cutty sark' (meaning short skirt) of the 'winsome wench' who chased the eponymous hero of the poem *Tam O'Shanter*, written by Robert Burns. The same witch, as a young girl, is the figurehead of the ship.

The *Cutty Sark* was built for the established sea master John Willis. Following a string of failures with his other vessels, his dream was to build a ship which would be fast enough to win the annual clipper's race to bring the new season's tea from China to London.

Scott & Linton, a Dumbarton firm, were commissioned to build this ship, of a size which they had never built before. Due to the magnitude of the project, they were keen to serve Willis to the best of their ability, but the combination of this eagerness and Willis's determination to pay them as little as possible for their efforts, resulted in the collapse of the company. It was Hercules Linton who designed the revolutionary new hull shape. Another company, William Denny & Brothers took over in the final stages of the ship's completion.

The *Cutty Sark*'s initial performances were good, but she never distinguished herself as the superior vessel of her master's

'But Tam kend what was what fu' brawlie:
There was ae winsome wench and wawlie,
That night enlisted in the core,
Lang after kend on Carrick shore
(For monie a beast to dead she shot,
An' perish'd monie a bonie boat,
And shook baith meikle corn and bear,
And kept the country-side in fear.)
Her cutty sark, o' Paisley harn,
That while a lassie she had worn,
In longitude tho' sorely scanty,
It was her best, and she was vauntie. . .'
— ROBERT BURNS, *TAM O'SHANTER*

dreams. Moreover she was only to sail on the China Tea Trade for a few seasons for, as she was making her first voyages, the times were already changing and the need for sailing ships was becoming increasingly redundant with the growing use of steamer trading, and the opening of the Suez Canal. Using sailing ships to carry cargos of tea was no longer profitable, and the *Cutty Sark* carried her last cargo of tea in 1877, less than ten years after her launch.

The *Cutty Sark* was used intermittently in the years between 1877 and 1885, but she was to prove herself conclusively during the era of the flourishing Australian wool trade. During this time, she was captained expertly by Richard Woodget, and frequently covered the water from Australia to England in the fastest time.

When she ceased to make any more money carrying wool, the *Cutty Sark* was sold to the Portuguese for whom she sailed as the training ship *Fereirra*, carrying colonial possessions, for the following thirty years. In 1916, she lost her mast in a storm in the Indian Ocean, and was re-rigged as a barquentine and renamed *Mario de Ambaro*.

In 1922, it was necessary for her to undergo a refit in London's Surrey Docks, but returning home she was driven by gales into Falmouth Harbour. Here she was seen by Captain Wilfred Dowman who had admired her in her glory days of the 1890s, and who consequently purchased her from the Portuguese. He restored and re-rigged the rundown ship and presented her as a stationary training ship in Falmouth.

On Dowman's death in 1938, the *Cutty Sark* was given by his widow to the Incorporated Thames Nautical Training College, where she remained until 1949. No longer needed by the cadets, who were beginning to train on the larger, steel ships, the *Cutty Sark* was moved to Greenwich. She remained on a mooring there until the formation of the Cutty Sark Society which decided to turn her into a museum ship and place her in a permanent dry dock. This occurred in 1954, and she was officially opened in 1957 by The Queen.

The Cutty Sark was, at one time, one of the fastest ships on the sea

Dartmoor National Park

In recognition of its outstanding natural beauty, Dartmoor, within the county of Devon, was declared as one of the National Parks of England and Wales in 1951. Its magnificent landscape and wooded valleys cover an area of 953 km² (368 miles²), thereby crediting Dartmoor with the widest area of open countryside in the south of England. Approximately 33,000 people live in Dartmoor, and it is estimated that over 10,000,000 people visit the area each year.

Dartmoor's landscape is stunning, and it provides wonderful terrain for walking and hiking. There is a variety of routes on the High Moor and in the valleys, and during the summer months the most popular paths become very animated. Most of the park lies over a granite plateau, 600 m (1,968 ft) above sea level, but it also encompasses areas of the neighbouring Devon countryside. The valley of the river Dart, after which the moor is named, runs through the granite plateau, its West and East rivers merging at Dartmeet. The surface of the plateau is broken up by tall, granite tors, of which there are estimated to be over 160. The highest of these is the High Willays Tor, which stands at 621 m (2,037 ft) above sea level. On the park's moorland, sheep, cattle and the famous Dartmoor ponies graze.

Princetown, home of the infamous maximum security prison, is Dartmoor's highest settlement at 420 m (1,377 ft). The construction of the prison was an initiative aimed at creating more employment within the area at the end of the eighteenth century.

In contrast to the truly stunning countryside, Dartmoor also features some of the wildest and bleakest landscapes in Britain, not traditionally picturesque, but mysteriously beautiful. Dartmoor's climate is cool and wet, dominated by south-westerly winds, and the combination of mist, rain and fog which can descend upon the park within minutes, often gives the area an eerie appearance. *The Hound of the Baskervilles*, the tale of Arthur Conan Doyle's Holmesian nemesis, was set in Dartmoor and was apparently based on a local legend.

In addition to being one of the most naturally beautiful of Britain's landscapes, Dartmoor is also an extremely important archaeological landscape, littered as it is with Bronze Age remains and artefacts. It is estimated that there has been human activity on Dartmoor since circa 10,000BC, when it is believed that the first clearings were made in the forest. There have been rare finds of flint tools which would have been

The famous Dartmoor Ponies have roamed the moor for many centuries

used between 8000 and 4000BC, but there are in fact very few remains which can be traced further back than 2500BC. Many features of Bronze Age life are reflected in the structures scattered throughout the moor. These include burial mounds and places believed to be of religious worship, fields, farms and huts. The remains, usually the large doorway stones, of over 5,000 Bronze Age huts have been located on Dartmoor.

Burial places were marked by cairns and tumuli, and over a thousand of these, in varying forms, are still visible. Also assumed to be associated with burial or religious ceremonies are the rows and circles of upright stones, which appear throughout Dartmoor, but their purpose is not clear.

As the climate changed across Dartmoor towards the end of the Bronze Age, the settlements moved further down to the lower ground, where the soil was less acidic and the weather less hostile. This movement away from the High Moor is the explanation usually given for the survival of so many of the artefacts which remain, as they lay relatively untouched for centuries. The durability of the structures can also be accredited to the fact that they were made from rough granite, an extremely durable stone.

As an area rich in natural resources, Dartmoor saw the construction of many mines and quarries. The stone used on Nelson's Column in Trafalgar Square was taken from Haytor in Dartmoor. As a consequence of the wealth amassed by the mining on Dartmoor, the area was able to build the attractive churches and buildings which we see today.

Dickens's House

Number 48 Doughty Street is the last remaining residence of the great British Victorian novelist Charles Dickens, who lived in the property, for £80 per year, for only two years between 1837 and 1839. It was within these walls that, amidst bouts of anxiety regarding his financial situation and his ever-growing family, Dickens produced some of his most well-known novels, including *The Pickwick Papers*, *Nicholas Nickleby* and *Oliver Twist*.

Dickens's time at Doughty Street was extremely prosperous, and it is partly this success which contributed to the brevity of his residence there. When his third child was born in 1839 the need for the family to move to more spacious accommodation became clear. As a result of his continued literary successes, Dickens was able to cater for this need, and the family moved to a house in Regents Park at the end of 1839.

The house held memories of both extreme joy and sadness for Dickens. His happiness was reflected in the huge volumes of work which he produced there and which brought him acclaim, but it was also in the house at Doughty Street that Dickens's sister-in-law, Mary Hogarth, whom Dickens dearly loved, and with whom he was extremely close, passed away. The room in which she died has been named the Mary Hogarth Room and is open to the public.

Dickens's wife Catherine, also benefited from her time in Doughty Street, for it was here where she wrote and consequently published her own cookery book.

Although Dickens's life in the house was short, the importance of the building as the only surviving property of the many in which Dickens resided throughout his life was recognised, and on the verge of demolition in 1923, the house was rescued by the Dickens Fellowship. This body, which had been in existence since 1902, gathered the money necessary to buy the freehold, and undertook the necessary renovations to the property. On completion of these in 1925, and under the control of an independent trust, the house was officially opened as The Dickens House Museum.

The house has been carefully repaired by the Fellowship, and the rooms have been restored to closely resemble those in which Dickens would have lived and worked. Exhibitions and galleries are devoted to his life and works, and a great variety of items are on display, including many of his own personal belongings.

All four storeys of the house are open to the public, and each room has been decorated with furniture and belongings which Dickens acquired throughout his life, and which were subsequently transferred to Doughty Street.

The house is not exactly as it would have been in Dickens's own time there. The library on the lower ground floor was actually the kitchen when Dickens was in residence. In its new capacity as a library its shelves are filled with collections of Dickens's works. Dickens and his wife were enthusiastic hosts, and many of the rooms in the house were used frequently for entertaining, notably the dining room where Dickens vivaciously presided over dinner parties.

The morning room offers a detailed account of Dickens's family history. Family portraits hang from the walls, as does the Dickens Family Tree, recorded by Dickens's great, great grandson. More personal items of family history are also on display. These include the engagement ring which Dickens gave to Catherine, his parents' family bible, and a single rose which was laid on his body on June 9, 1870, the day that he died.

Charles Dickens 1812–1870

Dover Castle

Due to its strategic location commanding the shortest sea route across the English Channel to mainland Europe, the town of Dover has, throughout its history, been an obvious target for invasion, and for centuries Dover Castle played a vital role in the defence of the country. Described in the thirteenth century as the 'Key of England', the castle is one of the largest in Britain, and it is believed that the remains of some of the fortifications which have been found on its site date back to the Iron Age.

Little is known about the first castle which was built at Dover. Its construction was ordered by William the Conqueror, then Duke of Normandy, prior to the Battle of Hastings in 1066, and it appears that it was built around the Roman lighthouse, pharos, the oldest lighthouse in Britain, believed to date back to the first century.

A century later, between 1179 and 1188, the main fortifications of Dover Castle were completely rebuilt by Henry II. The keep was built inside the inner bailey, and work commenced on the defences of the outer bailey, although these fortifications were not to be completed until the subsequent reign of King John. One of the most interesting features of the castle is the concentric arrangement of the fortifications, believed to be one of the first examples of such a design in England.

The castle withstood its first attack in 1216 when Prince Louis invaded England with an army from France in support of the rebel barons against King John. Within four months of this invasion, Dover was one of only two castles remaining in the south of England which had not been taken over by the French, and which still remained the property of the King. Louis's attack against Dover had been mainly directed from the French camp to the north of the castle. While his men tunnelled under the northern barbican, Louis bombarded the outer walls with stones. As a result of the mining, the eastern gate tower collapsed, thereby opening the castle up to the French who flooded in. The defenders of the castle, led by Hubert de Burgh, valiantly fought back and forced the French into retreat. In May 1217, Prince Louis attacked again and besieged Dover Castle, but only three days later the war was brought to a conclusion by the defeat of the French forces at Lincoln.

King John had died shortly after the first attack on Dover in October 1217 and was succeeded by his son Henry III who, having seen the near loss of the castle to the French, began a huge effort to fortify the site and strengthen the castle's defences. The work undertaken was extensive, and once completed, had greatly strengthened the power of the castle.

Centuries passed without incident at the castle, until the outbreak of Civil War in 1642. Cromwell's troops surprised the defenders of the castle, and seized it almost effortlessly. A century later, further additions were made to the castle to prepare it for the accommodation of extra troops, and the installation of heavy artillery. It was also considerably modernised and fortified against invasion during the Napoleonic Wars at the end of the eighteenth century. The potential of all available space within the castle was maximised, and a gateway was constructed for ease of movement between town and castle defences. Cavernous shelters were also built into the White Cliffs capable of hiding a large part of the British army in the event of an unexpected French attack.

During the nineteenth century the castle underwent another series of reinforcements and barrack building, but it was in the twentieth century, in the First and Second World Wars, that the castle was to play its next important role. It was fitted with searchlights and anti-aircraft guns in order to help the Dover Patrol control the Straits, and suffered much bomb damage and shelling. The operation to evacuate almost 340,000 Allied soldiers from Dunkirk was controlled from the underground barracks of Dover Castle. An underground hospital was built, as well as a headquarters for the army, navy and airforce. At the conclusion of the Second World War, the army stayed in the castle, and remained there until 1958 when the castle became the property of the Ministry of Works to whom the task of its preservation was awarded.

Durham Cathedral

The approaching view of Durham Cathedral, built on a peninsular carved out by the river Wear, dominates the city's skyline, and is an exceptionally beautiful sight. The Cathedral looms over its surroundings, and casts its shadow on to the wooded banks of the river below.

The first construction on the site where the Cathedral now stands was the Saxon White Church, in which a shrine was built for the body of St. Cuthbert by the community of monks who had formerly resided in Lindisfarne. It is believed that Cuthbert was born in the third decade of the seventh century. Throughout his life he took on the roles of monk, solitary and bishop, but he was famed in his time as a miracle worker. He died on Farne Island in 687, where it is believed that his body lay until 875 when the monks were forced to evacuate following the Danish raids which threatened their community. The monks placed Cuthbert's body in a coffin and carried him with them, resting at many sites, but eventually enshrining it in Uchted's minster church at Durham in 995.

The Norman bishop, William St. Carileph, replaced the Conqueror's appointee, William Walcher, who was murdered at Gateshead in 1081. Carileph refounded a monastery on the site of the church in 1092, and laid down the foundations for Durham Cathedral in the following year. His designs took approximately forty years to complete, and the resulting construction has changed very little in over eight centuries since.

The tomb of St. Cuthbert was moved into the Cathedral upon its completion, and some argue that this was indeed the only reason for the Cathedral's construction. The tomb still lies on the site of the original shrine of the White Church, now at the east end of Durham Cathedral.

Only two major additions were undertaken after the completion of Bishop William's original cathedral. The first of these was the construction of the Galilee Chapel, at the end of the twelfth century, by Bishop Hugh Le Puiset, and the second was the construction of the Chapel of

The Sanctuary Knocker on the North Door

Nine Altars, between 1242 and 1274, by Bishop Richard Le Poore.

It is perhaps fitting that a second tomb housed in the Cathedral is that of the Venerable Bede. An intelligent and prolific writer, Bede (673–735) celebrated the life of St. Cuthbert in a published work. His tomb lies in the Galilee Chapel, moved there in 1370, and is commemorated by a dark marble grave stone.

During the Middle Ages, the Cathedral served as a sanctuary for criminals fleeing their fate. Offenders would bang on the door using the Sanctuary Knocker and be admitted into the Cathedral for a maximum period of 37 days. During this time, they had to confess their crime to the coroner, and exchange their clothes for a black robe bearing the yellow cross of St. Cuthbert. At the end of their period of sanctuary, cared for and fed at the expense of the church, the criminal was escorted to an assigned port, where they were forced to leave the country. If they attempted escape en route, or refused to leave, they were executed.

Being home to the shrine of St. Cuthbert, Durham Cathedral became an important centre of pilgrimage, and during the medieval period the tomb was ornately decorated with jewels and gifts left by all those who visited it. Amongst the pilgrims who payed homage were nobility, royalty and senior churchmen.

Durham Cathedral suffered comparatively little damage during Henry VIII's dissolution of the monasteries, but the riches from the tomb of St. Cuthbert were found and confiscated, leaving only the plain tomb as it remains today. Vandals attacked the Cathedral at the end of the sixteenth century, and it suffered further damage in 1650 when the 3,000 Scottish prisoners, captured by Cromwell at the Battle of Dunbar, began to burn the woodwork of their Cathedral prison in order to keep warm.

Although having undergone some restoration schemes during the seventeenth and nineteenth centuries, some being necessary renovations, and some purely aesthetic alterations, the Cathedral has been extremely well preserved, and stands as a fine example of Norman architecture in the Romanesque style.

HAC SUNT IN FOSSA BEDAE VENERABILIS OSSA
In this tomb are the bones of the Venerable Bede

Eden Project

The Eden Project began as the desire to demonstrate the reliance of human beings on the plants around them. It is now a hugely ambitious experiment aimed at recreating climatic environments and exploring issues of sustainability on a global scale. This phenomenal undertaking was the brainchild of Tim Smit, now chief executive of Eden, who had previously been heavily involved in the uncovering and restoration of the Victorian Lost Gardens of Heligan. In total, the completion of the project spanned seven years, from its conception in 1994 to its full opening to the public in 2001, and cost approximately £86,000,000.

The Eden Project is located just outside St. Austell in Cornwall, and the site itself is a deep clay pit. Such a location was viewed as ideal by Eden's creator as the cliffs provided protection from the wind, and the 'greenhouses' could be built on the south-facing slopes which would store the heat which they attracted from the sun.

One of the many statues in the grounds of the Eden Project

A huge team of people was enlisted to build the Eden Project. In addition to the obviously necessary horticulturalists, architects and engineers, Smit also recruited artists and sculptors.

The initial plan for the project was the construction of two biomes, one recreating the environment of the humid tropics, and the other imitating a warm temperate climate. Plants more suited to cool temperate climates would be grown in the extensive outdoor gardens.

The question of how these biomes were to be designed and in which material they were to be constructed was one which required careful attention. A heavy glass and steel roof would require massive supports, which would potentially block some of the light to the plants thereby making them grow unnaturally tall in their quest for the sun's energy. The answer was to build a geodesic dome, a dome comprising of many flat straight-sided surfaces which intersect to form a curved shape, and to construct it from ETFE, a strain of fluoropolymer. An ETFE panel weighs one hundredth of its glass equivalent, as well as being strong with a high transparency to UV light, yet not degraded by it.

The two biomes each consist of four domes, and the intersections at which they join are strengthened by steel arches. The humid tropics is the larger of the two, and it covers an area of 15,793 m² (170,000 ft²), with a height of 55 m (180 ft). It has been calculated that it is big enough to house the Tower of London. The warm temperate biome covers 6,503 m² (70,000 ft²), and reaches a height of 35 m (115 ft).

The scaffolding required to erect the huge biomes was itself record-breaking, and entered the Guinness Book of Records as the world's highest freestanding structure.

The temperature and humidity within the biomes is monitored electronically. Openings at the top and bottom of the domes are controlled by a computer which circulates hot air from the top, or cool air from the bottom as necessary. The total estimated annual water requirement of the project is 16,000,000 gallons.

Already a huge success, with visitor figures in their millions and a rating of Britain's third most popular attraction, the Eden Project is planning to extend its environmental showcase further with the proposed construction of a third biodome. This third dome will recreate the arid regions of the dry tropics, in particular exploring desert plants and human survival in areas of little water.

Edinburgh Castle

Edinburgh Castle, presiding majestically over the capital city of Scotland from its location high on an extinct volcanic outcrop, is one of Scotland's leading tourist attractions, and a dominant national symbol. Much of the story of the castle is effectively the story of Scotland itself.

Evidence suggests that there has been human activity on the castle rock dating back to the Bronze Age. At 135m (442ft) above sea level, the location was an obvious choice for the construction of a stronghold. There are traces of occupation in the sixth century, but the first documented fort on the site was Din Eidyn, in the seventh century, occupied by the local Celtic tribe. King Edwin and the Northumbrians invaded the south east of Scotland in 638, and some believe that therein lies the origin of the city's name as it is now known - Edwin's Burgh.

A stone fort was built on the rock at the end of the eleventh century by Malcolm III. When his wife Margaret (later canonised) died in 1093, it is believed that her son, King David, built the tiny chapel which now bears her name on the rock's highest point. It is the oldest building in the area of the castle, and barely escaped demolition on a number of occasions.

Ownership of the castle changed hands quite frequently during the eleventh to thirteenth centuries. The captured King William the Lion was forced to sacrifice Edinburgh Castle and three others in return for his ransom in 1174, but Edinburgh was recaptured in 1186. In the period during 1296-1342, the Wars of Independence, Robert the Bruce was so surprised at the ease with which the castle was captured and recaptured on four occasions that he tore down the fortifications as soon as the castle came back into his possession in 1314. In 1335, Edward III constructed a new castle but it stood for only six years.

The main period of construction began in 1368, a decade after the return of David II from captivity in England. This construction was to last 200 years. The first edifices were David's Tower, St. Mary's Church and a new gate tower. In 1434, work began on the Kings Great Chamber, and Holyrood House was completed in the following century.

Over the sixteenth and seventeenth centuries the castle sustained some serious damage as a result of sieges. The worst of these was the Lang siege in 1571. The entire front of the eastern block was destroyed by the regent Morton who had enlisted the help of the English and their artillery to force the keeper of the castle, Sir William Kirkcaldy, to surrender. After Kirkcaldy's surrender and consequent execution, reconstruction began immediately.

The next siege occurred in 1640, and this badly damaged the defences of the castle. In 1650 a three month siege led to the establishment of Oliver Cromwell's Scottish headquarters at the castle. He created an army, and what had previously been a royal castle became a garrison fortress, comprising of barracks, officers' quarters and storehouses. The last occasion on which the castle came under military attack occurred in 1745, when Prince Charles Edward Stuart made a lackadaisical and unsurprisingly unsuccessful attempt to take the castle on his march south.

One of the greatest discoveries in the castle was the finding of a locked chest which proved to contain the Honours of Scotland. These were discovered in the Crown Room in 1818, where they had been untouched since 1707. They were put on display immediately, and thus began the history of Edinburgh Castle as a tourist attraction. Also on display with the Honours of Scotland in the Crown Room is the Stone of Destiny, controversially retained in Westminster under the Coronation Chair, where it was placed by Edward I in 1301. It was equally controversially moved to Edinburgh Castle by Prime Minister John Major in 1996 even though it had come from Scone, and originally, in the dark ages, from Ireland.

Of the most visited buildings at the castle are St. Margaret's Chapel, and the small, wood-panelled room in the Royal Apartments in which Mary Queen of Scots gave birth to King James VI.

The Stone of Destiny being driven up the Royal Mile to be installed in Edinburgh Castle

Exmoor National Park

The smallest and most compact of the National Parks of England and Wales, Exmoor National Park covers an area of 686 km² (265 miles²), and encompasses parts of West Somerset and North Devon. The park's landscapes are varied and beautiful, and the views from its coastline extend out across the Bristol Channel. Wild red deer, ancient oak woodland and breathtaking scenery are all distinctive features of Exmoor National Park.

Exmoor is a high sandstone plateau, cut by deep valleys and fast-flowing rivers, the two largest of which are the Exe and the Barle. It has smooth curved hillsides, and open moors, often beautifully shrouded in mist and fog.

Several attractive villages are also located within Exmoor. These include Porlock on the moor's edge, Lynton and Lynmouth which are linked by a water-operated cliff railway. Interesting buildings include the partly medieval castle of Dunster, and the traditional thatched cottages of Selworthy. With the exception of Selworthy, and the inclusion of Dulverton and Exford, these towns and villages are Exmoor's main centres.

Evidence exists of early human settlement at Exmoor, but this appears to have been restricted to the areas around Exmoor, excluding the moor itself. Stone circles can be seen at Porlock Hill and Almsworthy Common which date back to around 1800–1500BC. Also believed to be from this period are the standing stones and 350 burial mounds. Barrow clusters, like the eleven Chapman Barrows, are common.

Remains can be found on Exmoor from settlements throughout the ages. Iron Age hill forts can be seen at Shoulsbarrow Castle, Road Castle and Staddon Hill Camp. Roman occupation left fewer artefacts, only the fortlets at Old Barrow and the Beacon are still visible. There are inscribed stones from the Dark Ages, and examples of defensive earthworks from the Norman and Medieval periods. The most significant example of this is the grass-covered motte and bailey earthwork at Holwell Castle.

One of the most controversial yet most well-known of Exmoor's monuments is the Tarr Steps, a medieval clapper bridge over the river Barle. Some believe that this dates back to the Bronze Age, perhaps indicated by the presence of Bronze Age burial mounds, whereas others believe they are as recent as 1400.

Although a large percentage of Exmoor is privately owned, the area still offers spectacular walks, and it is estimated that there are over 160 km (100 miles) of walking paths. The National Trust owns many areas of Exmoor and distributes literature detailing the recommended walks throughout the park. Dukerry Beacon, at 519 m (1,702 ft), is the highest point in Exmoor, and is located in the Holnicote Estate, owned by the National Trust.

The beauty of Exmoor has served as a source of inspiration for many novelists who have been to visit. The scenery is described so accurately by R.D. Blackmore in *Lorna Doone* that the places depicted are still recognisable today, and a track in the countryside which stirred Henry Williamson to write *Tarka the Otter* has now been retrospectively named the Tarka Trail.

The bestowal of National Park status upon Exmoor is an attempt to preserve the landscapes, wildlife and history in an area of beauty and tranquillity on an increasingly overcrowded island. It is also a place to be lived in and enjoyed, and is home to over 10,500 people.

Exmoor is home to a remarkable variety of flora and rare wildlife, including red deer, wild ponies and several birds of prey

Fishbourne Roman Palace

The fortuitous discovery of the impressive remains of the Roman site at Fishbourne in Chichester occurred in 1960 as the ground was being dug up in order to install a new water main. This discovery was to become one of the most important British archaeological finds of the twentieth century, and thus began nine seasons of excavations.

From these excavations, archaeologists traced the development of the site through three distinct chapters. The first chapter began with a construction that dates back to the time of the Roman invasion in 43, and consisted of two granary stores supported on wooden piles. Military equipment was found surrounding the remains of this structure, indicating that the site had been used as a military base.

It appears however, that this military base was soon abandoned, and the constructions taken apart, to be replaced with a timber dwelling containing twelve rooms, the smallest of which are believed to have been allocated to the servants. This wooden structure was in turn dismantled in 65–75, and a more highly crafted stone building took its place.

The site entered its third and final chapter in 75 with the construction of the Flavian Palace, the remains of which are still visible today. The Palace would have been extremely elaborate, even matching the sizes of the imperial palaces in Rome. The main entrance to the palace would have been at the eastern end of its four wings, which were built symmetrically around a central courtyard. Inside, the building contained an audience chamber, the essential Roman bathhouse and a series of room suites. The main approach to the palace would have been across the gardens, with an ornate hedge marking the path on either side.

The combination of the traditional plan of the building, the detailed architecture and the excellence of the workmanship demonstrates that a significant amount of money was expended on this project. Some believe that the palace was constructed for the Celtic king, Tiberius Claudius Togidubnus, and it is possible that Fishbourne is actually the site of the first invasion.

Evidence suggests that work continued on the palace for the following 200 years. Most of the work appears to have been aesthetic, with ornate decorations added to the ceilings and walls, and the laying of the beautiful mosaic floors, some of which were laid over earlier works.

Large areas of the palace however, were destroyed in the third century, when it appears that a serious fire broke out. Work was not continued, and repairs were not undertaken, and the once beautiful palace simply fell down. The only subsequent activity on the site was in the fourth and fifth centuries, as testified by the Saxon burials discovered in the remains of the site.

Today, of the palace's original four wings, only one, the northern wing can be viewed. The mosaics in this part of the palace are extraordinary, and the virtually complete work entitled Cupid on a Dolphin (right), which contains around 360,000 pieces is one of the most remarkable examples of this type of art in Britain. The gardens have been recreated to resemble the gardens in Roman times, and from these, the true size of Fishbourne Roman Palace can be appreciated. Also on display in the gardens are the plants which would have been grown by the Romans, a Roman Garden Museum and a collection of original and replica horticultural tools which would have been used on the site.

A model to show how Fishbourne Roman Palace may have appeared almost 2000 years ago

Forth Railway Bridge

The Forth Railway Bridge is one of the most spectacular man-made landmarks in Scotland, and a monument to civil engineering. The total length of the bridge is 2,522 m (8,276 ft), and it is composed of 54,000 tonnes of steel, 194,000 cubic yards of granite, stone and concrete. Between 6–7,000,000 rivets hold the structure in place.

When the proposal for a railway link between the opposing banks of the River Forth was submitted, the first suggestion was the construction of a tunnel. This idea was short-lived however, as on careful consideration the conclusion was reached that a tunnel would be unsafe. The alternative solution was the construction of a bridge.

In 1818 a number of designs were presented, but none were acceptable, and it was not until 1865 that parliament commissioned the engineer Thomas Bouch, of the North British Railway, to build the Forth Railway Bridge. Bouch was a respected engineer and had been responsible for the construction of the bridge over the river Tay.

Had tragedy not struck in December 1879, then it is likely that Bouch's design of a suspended bridge over Forth would have been implemented, but when the news came in that the Tay Bridge had collapsed in a hurricane, killing 75 passengers travelling on the Edinburgh train, Bouch's reputation was shattered and his design, and indeed very involvement in the project, cancelled immediately.

Realising that the shaken Scottish public would need reassurance in the form of a bridge which would appear as if it could never fall down, engineers Sir John Fowler and Benjamin Baker offered the perfect structural solution. They presented a design which was proving to be popular on a global scale, the cantilever bridge.

The contract was awarded in December 1882, and eight years later the bridge was completed. The Forth Railway Bridge was indeed one of the strongest bridges ever built, but with such quality came the price tag of a staggering £3,000,000. 5,000 workers were employed on the bridge, and of these, only 57 lost their lives while working on the project. With such a huge number of employees this was a safety record at the end of the nineteenth century.

Benjamin Baker, also responsible for the building of the London Underground and the transportation of the Cleopatra obelisk from Egypt to England, was duly knighted in 1890.

Although the Bridge had achieved its objectives of strength and purpose the design was not appreciated by some, and the poet and artist William Morris criticised the bridge for being 'the supremest specimen of all ugliness'. Aesthetically pleasing or not however, the Bridge is considered to be one of the industrial wonders of the world, and still stands solidly against the strongest of Scottish winds. Today, approximately 200 trains cross the Forth Railway Bridge per day.

In 1990, to celebrate the 100th anniversary of the Bridge, over 1000 lamps, running along 40 km (25 miles) of cables, were added to it.

The maintenance of the Bridge is strictly monitored and it has been conserved in a spectacular condition. Almost half of the budget for the bridge's maintenance is spent on painting. It is humorously believed that painting the Forth Railway Bridge is an infinite task, for in the time which it takes to reach the opposite end, repainting is necessary where the painting originally began.

One of the Bridge's legends is that of the Golden Rivet. It has been reported that one of the millions of rivets used in the construction of the bridge is actually made of solid gold. Whether or not this is true, it has also been reported that the golden rivet has now been removed, most likely an attempt to prevent any fortune hunters risking their lives in its quest.

'If I had pretended that the building of the Forth Bridge was not a source of constant anxiety, present and future, no experienced engineer would have believed me.'
– SIR BENJAMIN BAKER, 1840–1907

Giant's Causeway

Climbing up to the sky from the sea on the northern coast of County Antrim is a mysterious staircase of hexagonal basalt columns, Ireland's famous Giant's Causeway. Westwards, the Causeway stretches out to sea in the direction of Scotland, and its stepping stones gradually disappear beneath the surface of the water. For centuries, visitors have admired the splendour and arrangement of these mystifying stones, and speculated both scientifically and fantastically on their origins.

The debate on the formation of the Giant's Causeway dates back to the seventeenth century. The Bishop of Derry visited the area in 1692, and on seeing the Causeway, he circulated news of his discovery around the erudite assemblies of Dublin and subsequently London. The news caused much controversy, and in 1694, a paper on the Causeway's discovery and possible origins was submitted to the Royal Society in Dublin by Sir Richard Bulkely, a fellow of Trinity College. Theories were prolific but two main hypotheses emerged. To begin with, the view most commonly held was that the Causeway was the work of giants, but the theory which came to displace it was that the phenomenon had been naturally formed. Regardless of which theory was accurate, both were equally intriguing.

The Legend

Amongst those who commonly believe that the Causeway was the work of giants, or more specifically the work of Finn McCool, Ulster warrior and commander of the guardians of Ireland, opinions are still divided on how it was actually formed.

The romantic version of events is that Finn had fallen in love with a lady giant who lived on the island of Staffa in the Hebrides, and that the Causeway, leading as it does out to sea, was the beginning of a path, now underwater, which he built to facilitate his journey across the water to his love. This myth was supported by the presence on the island of Staffa of a similar formation of basalt columns leading out of the water.

A more heroic story is that of Finn's battle with a Scottish adversary. Finn was conducting his daily tasks in peace, when the Scottish giant began to antagonise him and criticise his fighting ability from across the water. In anger, Finn picked up a piece of land and threw it at the giant who then retaliated by doing the same. The Scottish giant declared that if only he could swim he would cross the channel and defeat Finn in a battle. Infuriated, Finn tore pieces of rock from the cliffs and threw them down one by one into the water forming a path which stretched from Ireland to Scotland. The frightened Scottish giant could not afford to lose face and began the journey across the water. By this time Finn was tired from making the Causeway, and devised a clever plan. He dressed himself up as a baby and made a large cot in which he lay down and awaited the Scottish giant. When the Scottish giant thundered through the door shouting for McCool, his eyes fell upon the 'baby' and he was terrified. If what he saw was a mere baby, then he was not prepared to meet its father. McCool jumped out of the cot and loomed above the giant, who turned on his heels and ran back over the Causeway, breaking every single stone on his way, to the safety of Scotland.

The Scientific Theory

The formation of the Causeway occurred approximately sixty million years ago during the early Tertiary period when Antrim was subject to intense igneous activity. Highly fluid molten rock was forced up through the cracks and openings of the chalk bed and would have formed a far-reaching lava plateau. Three of these lava outflows occurred and they came to be classed as the Lower, Middle and Upper Basaltic. The periods of quiet activity between them are evident from the different layers which have formed.

The columns of the Giant's Causeway are formed by the Middle Basalt rocks, a result of variations in the rate at which the lava cooled and contracted, and consequently cracked the resulting rock into the even blocks seen there today.

In an age where very little escapes scientific explanation, it seems surprising that the theory of lovesick or warring giants could have been seriously supported, but on sight of the spectacular Giant's Causeway such a liberation of imagination almost becomes understandable.

Glasgow Cathedral

In the heart of Scotland's largest city, Glasgow Cathedral stands as a proud example of Medieval Scotland's finest buildings. It is a well preserved cathedral, and is the only mainland Scottish cathedral to have survived the Reformation, suffering only the loss of its western towers.

The ground on which the Cathedral stands has been hallowed since 397, when it was dedicated as a Christian burial ground by St. Ninian. In the following century St. Kentigern, often referred to as Mungo, the first bishop within the ancient British kingdom of Strathclyde, came to Glasgow to bury the body of a holy man from Stirlingshire. He brought the body to the city on a cart led by oxen, and buried the body in St. Ninian's burial ground. He then remained in Glasgow, and was subsequently elected by the king and clergy to be their bishop, and following this appointment he founded a monastic community and built a church in the city.

Kentigern is believed to have died in 603, and although he had

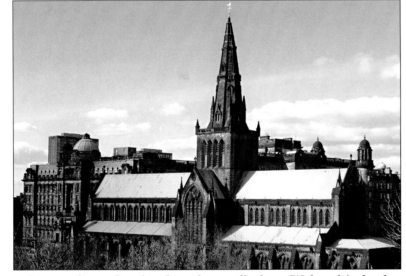

moved away from Scotland and travelled to Wales, his body was brought back and his tomb is in the Lower Church of the Cathedral, where a light continually burns. The colourful silk cloth which covers his tomb, and the six kneelers, were dedicated before Princess Margaret in 1973. This shrine is the focal point of the cathedral, and every year a service is held to commemorate St. Kentigern's life.

There are no detailed records of the buildings which existed on the site of the present Cathedral, but the first stone building was consecrated in 1136. This was done in front of an audience which included King David I and his court. The building stood for 60 years until it was destroyed by fire, whereupon a larger cathedral was constructed in its place.

In the early thirteenth century an extension was made to the Nave, and the south-west door and entrance to the Blacader Aisle were installed. Major construction work began shortly afterwards, commissioned by William de Bondinton, adding the choir and the Lower Church. It is thought that the entire Cathedral was complete by the end of the thirteenth century. Additions and amendments however, were still being undertaken after this time and work continued up to, during and after the Reformation period, from which the cathedral famously emerged remarkably unscathed.

One of the most significant post-Reformation developments was the dividing wall introduced in the nave. This sectioned off the western end of the nave for worship exclusively by a congregation known as the Outer High. They worshipped there for almost 200 years from the mid-seventeenth century. Another congregation, the Barony, worshipped in the Lower Church from the end of the sixteenth century to the turn of the nineteenth century. When the Barony moved their congregation to a nearby church and ceased to employ the Lower Church as their place of worship, the area instead became the burial ground for the members of their congregation. It remained thus until the mid-nineteenth century when the area was cleared.

The twentieth century has seen a number of restorative measures undertaken to the cathedral, and the addition of many new features to it. The great East Window, which depicts the four evangelists, was installed in the choir in 1951, six years before re-crafted pews and stalls were introduced as replacements of those originally dating from the mid-nineteenth century. Major work has also been carried out on the cathedral precinct, in which are located the Museum of World Religions and Provand's Lordship, Glasgow's oldest house.

Glastonbury Abbey

The myths and legends which envelope Glastonbury and its Abbey tell a story of the mythical Avalon and the ancient Arthurian legends, of Joseph of Arimathea and the early Saints. It is claimed that Glastonbury has been occupied since the first century, yet there is, unfortunately, no evidence to support this.

The county of Somerset, in which Glastonbury lies, was conquered by the Saxons in the seventh century, and the first definite traces of the Abbey date back to this time when the king, Ine of Wessex, gave a charter to a monastery and erected a stone church on the site.

This church grew in importance and was enlarged under the abbacy of St. Dunstan, who later became Archbishop of Canterbury. The acquired wealth of the Abbey however, was not sufficient to save the Saxon monks from the Norman invasion and conquest of England. Under the Normans, and more exactly the first Norman Abbot, Turstin, the Abbey was improved and built upon, with magnificent structures added. Such was the work and effort put into the Abbey that when, in 1086, the census was taken and records made of life in England, Glastonbury Abbey proved to be the most affluent monastery in the country. This status was not to last long however, for fire destroyed much of the Abbey in 1184.

The most prominent remains of the Abbey today are the two great columns which stand where the nave and chancel meet, and the Lady Chapel, the ruins of which stand on the grounds of the Saxon church and date back to the late twelfth century. This suggests that the Lady Chapel was built immediately after the fire in 1184. The Chapel appears to have been elaborately decorated with sculptured doorways and Norman architectural ornamentation. The main monastic buildings still visible are the gatehouse and the abbot's kitchen, which dates back to the fourteenth century. The kitchen is the most intact of its kind in Europe and displays strong evidence of the power and wealth of Glastonbury's abbot.

Somewhat overshadowing the factual history of the Abbey however, are the mystical tales of Avalon, the holy grail and King Arthur for which Glastonbury is famed world-wide. The mysterious Glastonbury Tor, which rises to 152 m (500 ft), is the source of much speculation. When the sea came inland and surrounded the base of the hills of Glastonbury 2,000 years ago, this enchanting island, named Avalon after the Celtic God of the Underworld, was believed to be the meeting place of not only sea and land, but also of the dead. From here, the dead could finally depart from earth.

Legend has it that it was to the island of Avalon that Joseph of Arimathea carried the cup from which Jesus had drunk at the Last

The mysterious Glastonbury Tor

Supper. This was the Holy Grail, the sacred vessel in which Joseph had caught Jesus's blood during the crucifixion, and from which the gift of eternal youth would be granted to whomsoever drank of its contents. In quest of this Holy Grail, crusades were launched across England, Europe and the Far East, and it was supposedly in quest of the cup that King Arthur and the Knights of the Round Table came to Glastonbury.

Driven by the belief that the body of King Arthur lay in the graveyard of Glastonbury Abbey, the Abbey's monks excavated Arthur's supposed burial site in 1191. They claimed to have found a cross bearing the inscription, HIC IACET SEPULTUS INCLITUS REX ARTURIUS IN INSULA AVALONIA, *Here lies buried the renowned King Arthur in the Isle of Avalon.* Bones were secretly removed from the site and placed in caskets where they remained until 1278 when they were transferred, overseen by Edward I, to a marble tomb before the high altar of the Abbey church. When Henry VIII issued his orders of the dissolution of the monasteries, Glastonbury Abbey and its contents were destroyed. Arthur's tomb disappeared and has never been seen again.

The stories about Arthur's grave and Joseph of Arimathea were however, almost certainly invented by the monks after the 1184 fire as a means of generating income for rebuilding. The 'pilgrimage industry' was the best way to achieve this, and the monks ploy was successful.

Gloucester Cathedral

A focal point in Gloucester, and one of the finest cathedrals in England, is Gloucester Cathedral, Church of St. Peter and the Holy and Indivisible Trinity. The city of Gloucester, mainly due to its location, was recognised as an important site by the Romans at the time of their occupation. They took over and developed an existing 'Celtic' castle and as a result of this, and its strategic trade routes, Gloucester continued to be the capital of a small dark age kingdom after the Romans departed.

Christianity was later revived in Gloucester when the Abbey of St. Peter was founded in 681. The wooden structure of the Abbey was replaced by stone two centuries later, and secular priests replaced religious ones. In the early tenth century a priory was built to house the relics of St. Oswald which had been brought to Gloucester by his daughter. In 1022, by order of Canute, Benedictine monks replaced the secular priests.

An external feature of Gloucester Cathedral

In 1058, Aldred, the Bishop of Worcester, whose predecessor had influenced Canute's decision to replace the existing priests, took charge of the Abbey and made some elaborate alterations and additions to the church. When the last Saxon Abbot died in 1072, Serlo, a Norman from the monastery at Mont-St. Michel, arrived to take over the church at Gloucester. His main aim was to elevate the status of the Abbey, and this he did. By the turn of the twelfth century he had increased the population of the Abbey ten-fold, and carried out the necessary renovations which accompanied its increased size.

In 1088, fire destroyed the building originally constructed by Aldred, and Serlo began construction of a new church, the foundation stone of which was laid in 1089. Much of Gloucester Cathedral's design was based on the cathedral at Worcester, the construction of which had begun only four years previously, and had itself followed the model of the Norman-style cathedrals on the European mainland.

Tragedy struck again only 22 years after the new building had been consecrated in 1100, and most of the Norman church was devastated. Financial difficulties slowed the progress of the repairs and much of the church's reconstruction was done by the monks themselves. The southern tower of the Abbey collapsed in 1170, and further problems were encountered when the monks were forced to sell many of their valuables to ransom by King Richard I, and the seizure of one-third of their property by King John thirteen years later. Nevertheless the renovations continued and in 1216 the cathedral was deemed suitable for the occasion of the coronation of King Henry III, an event which consequently renewed royal interest in the Abbey Church. Over the following century and a half the Abbey gained importance and by 1378, when Parliament was held there by Richard II, the Abbey was already a significant site of pilgrimage, following the burial there of the murdered King Edward II, as well as a feat of architectural construction.

Edward II had a significant posthumous impact on the fortunes of the cathedral. The revenue generated by the pilgrimages made to the cathedral financed the entire construction of the Chapel of St. Andrew. Noblemen and women donated items of great value in commemoration, and Edward III, in order to maintain a suitable resting place for his father, donated generously to the Abbey.

Henry VIII's Act of Supremacy and consequent dissolution of the monasteries threw the abbey into turmoil, and it surrendered in 1540. By 1541, the new diocese of Gloucester had been established and the abbey was declared a cathedral.

The cathedral's cloisters are one of its most striking features, and they are famed for the fantastic fan vaulting above all four of the walks, claimed to be the earliest, and indeed the finest, in Great Britain. The lives of the monks were based in the cloister area, for here they worked and prayed. This area of the cathedral served a very different purpose in the early part of this century when the cloisters became the film location for the interior shots of 'Hogwarts School' for the film production of *Harry Potter and the Philosopher's Stone* by J.K. Rowling.

Glyndebourne Opera House

On a May afternoon in 1934, travellers at Victoria Station in London were surprised to see a small party of men and women in evening attire boarding a train bound for East Sussex. The occasion was the opening of the first season of operatic performances at Glyndebourne, a season which began as a two week period and is now an internationally famous event, which runs annually from May until October.

John Christie had inherited the estate at Glyndebourne in 1920, and it was there that he had met his wife, the operatic soprano Audrey Mildmay, who had been invited to the estate to perfect one of the amateur operatic performances which John was staging in the Organ Room, then the centre of musical activity.

The newlyweds spent their honeymoon at the festivals of Salzburg and Bayreuth, and subsequently returned to their home overflowing with ideas for the creation of their own small theatre at the estate. John created several initial plans, but the final design of the theatre comprised of an orchestra pit and a stage fitted with the latest lighting equipment and technology, and an auditorium capable of holding 300 people.

The project was destined for success. Completed as it was in the pre-war years, Glyndebourne Opera House was one of the few beneficiaries of the Hitler regime. Carl Ebert and Fritz Busch, Glyndebourne's first artistic director and conductor respectively, were no longer able to work in Germany and had consequently left their homeland for England. Upon their arrival, they accepted the offered positions at the Opera House. This serendipity was followed by hard-earned success, and the opening performance of *Le Nozze di Figaro* overwhelmed its initially dubious audience. The experience was made even more enjoyable by the location of the Opera House in its scenic Sussex surroundings, and the lengthy interval which allowed for a champagne picnic to be enjoyed on the lawn in between acts.

John Christie, co-founder of the Glyndebourne Festival Opera

With each season came new additions, improvements and enlargements to the House and gardens, and also an extension of the company's repertoire, which had previously concentrated mainly on the works of Mozart. By 1939, Glyndebourne had truly made a name for itself, and was a recognised model for operatic style and standard.

The fortunes of Glyndebourne however, ground to a halt with the outbreak of the Second World War. Performances were cancelled and the house became a refuge for London's evacuees.

Although the war ended six years later, it was not until 1950 that John Christie was given the help he needed to restore Glyndebourne to its former glory. In the post-war years, Christie had had no money, having spent it all on the Opera House in its formative years. The Glyndebourne Festival Society was thus established and its first achievement was the introduction of subscription to each festival, thereby guaranteeing annual financial support. Two years later, the Glyndebourne Arts Council was formed. They established the award of a grant to the company, designed to fund the necessary maintenance and pay for any improvements or renovation to the property. These two bodies are credited with Glyndebourne's revival, and the preservation of its traditions and high standards.

By 1964, Busch, Mildmay and Christie had all passed away, and Carl Ebert had retired. Such had been the impact and influence of these four individuals that the loss to Glyndebourne was immense. As a result however, of the shining examples they had set, their successors at the Opera House were able to follow their lead and continued to further their achievements. In 1966, plans were announced to begin a touring company, and this venture has not only enjoyed enormous success but has also launched the careers of many of the young artists who have toured with it.

In the 1980s, it was recognised that the Opera House at Glyndebourne could no longer meet the demand in the number of people who wished to attend performances, and due to technical limitations, was also having difficulty coping with the more advanced productions. The resulting, award-winning new building was completed in 1994, and opened on the same day in May, with a performance of the same opera that it had done 60 years previously.

John Christie's Glyndebourne Estate

Hadrian's Wall

British resistance to the Roman invasion in 43 was spirited, yet sporadic and badly organised, and by the middle of the first century, the majority of England was under Roman rule. The north of England and the warlike people of Wales proved harder to control, but within 30 years these too were occupied by Rome. The Scots however, were relentless and brutal in the defence of their land, and their resolve to fight the Romans was unerringly strong. Continued attempts failed, and by the second century, the Emperor Hadrian reached the decision that in lieu of conquering Scotland, it would suffice simply to keep these northern Barbarians out of England, and thus in 122, he ordered a wall to be built which would stretch across the country.

Hadrian's Wall is widely considered to be the principal monument of the Roman occupation in Britain and the most outstanding of all Roman border constructions. From Wallsend-on-Tyne in the east the wall stretched 117 km (73 miles) westwards to Bowness on the Solway Firth, and at the highest point of its path it follows the ground to 347 m (1,230 ft) above sea level.

Built of stone and turf, and ranging in height from 3.6 m (12 ft) to 6 m (20 ft), the wall consisted of seventeen large forts at intervals of approximately 8 km (5 miles), and a line of smaller forts positioned regularly one Roman mile apart from each other. Two 6 m (20 ft) observation turrets were built in between each pair of the milecastles. Ditches were built to run infront of the wall to the north and south. The ditch on the northern side was approximately 8 m (27 ft) wide and 2.7 m (9 ft) deep, and the southern ditch, or *vallum*, had a width of 6 m (20 ft) and a depth of 3 m (10 ft), with earthworks built on either side.

The wall was an enormously ambitious engineering project, which by the time the Roman legions had completed the wall in 128, had necessitated the movement of two million cubic yards of soil.

Infantry and cavalry from all parts of the Empire were stationed at the forts and milecastles of the wall, and thus the Romans clearly established control of the border. It appears that these soldiers' primary functions were to monitor the movement of people across the border and to prevent minor raiding of the frontier. It seems unlikely that these garrisons could have prevented a well-organised and resolute attack on any single point of the Wall.

In 197 AD, Hadrian's Wall was abandoned, but it was rebuilt and soldiers were re-positioned at its forts. The same happened at the end of the thirteenth century. There are no definite records detailing the exact year when the Wall was finally deserted, but it is estimated to have been in the last 20 years of the fourth century, just before the Roman Empire fragmented.

Today it is mainly the foundations of this great Wall which are visible. Its stones were plundered to build a new road from Newcastle to Carlisle in 1745, and two centuries later 274 m (300 yards) of it was quarried for military use in the Second World War. The Wall is now a World Heritage Site, and tourists can visit the surviving sections of the Wall, and some of the milecastles, forts and turrets. Although mostly in ruins, the remaining visible structures in their magnificent surrounding landscape tell the story of the past glories of a great civilisation.

J.Chapman Sculp.

PUB. ÆL. ADRIAN.

Published as the Act directs May 20.th 1797 by J.Wilkes

Caesar Traianus Hadrianus Augustus, 76–138

Hampton Court Palace

Standing grandly by the River Thames, Hampton Court Palace is the largest and most magnificent of the Tudor structures which remain in England today. Although it is significantly close to London, and for this reason is steeped in historical importance, the beauty of the palace and its surrounding gardens remove it from the capital city completely.

The construction of the Palace was begun by Cardinal Wolsey, the Archbishop of York and subsequently Cardinal and Lord Chancellor of England, after securing the lease in 1514. In order to create a palace befitting a man of his status, Wolsey made ambitious plans and the Palace was soon undergoing major building work. No expense was spared and the scale of the construction was phenomenal.

Wolsey both lived and worked in Hampton Court Palace, using it equally for pleasure and for affairs of state. His residency there however, was to be short-lived for by 1528, having failed to secure the divorce of Henry VIII and Catherine of Aragon, which the monarch was so desperately seeking from the Pope, Wolsey fell quickly from favour. In an attempt to sweeten the relations between the King and himself, Wolsey offered the palace to Henry as a gift. Henry accepted, but this did not save Wolsey who was charged with high treason in 1530, but died before his trial.

The size and splendour of Hampton Court Palace rendered it an extremely suitable palace for royalty, and so it remained until the death of George II in 1760. Henry VIII added to and altered the palace, obscuring much of Wolsey's original construction. Among the extensions built by Henry were the Great Hall, the Chapel and the extensive kitchens. It is estimated that in just under a decade, he spent the modern-day equivalent of £18,000,000 on renovations and extensions. In 1540, Hampton Court Palace was complete and was a proud example of modernity and sophistication.

No significant alterations were made to the palace for almost a century and a half until William III ascended the throne in 1689. William did not enjoy living in London, and employed the architect Sir Christopher Wren to enlarge the palace further to make it a suitable alternative to his London residence of Whitehall Palace. Wren's original plan to completely demolish and rebuild the Tudor Palace, with the exception of the Great Hall, fell short of both time and money and the revised plans consisted of only the rebuilding of the King and Queen's apartments on the south and east sides. Further designs included the cloistered Fountain Court, and the Cartoon Gallery, which displays the great tapestry designs by Raphael. Wren also decorated the Chapel. William did not live long to enjoy his new palace, and when he died in a riding accident in 1702 there were no further significant changes to the building.

Subsequent monarchs lived in Hampton Court Palace, but with George III's expressed preference for Windsor Castle came the end of the royal residence at Hampton Court, and all aspects of royal life were removed.

Although royal interest in the palace had waned, architects and historians demonstrated a keen enthusiasm to restore the building to its original Tudor glory. When the stage and seating of the Great Hall was removed at the end of the eighteenth century, the architecture of the Tudor interior was once again visible. A programme of Victorian restoration followed in the mid-nineteenth century and the palace was remodelled in the Tudor style.

The Palace survived the two World Wars, remaining virtually undamaged. In the 1970s and '80s, the Palace's potential as a visitor attraction was recognised, improvements were made and exhibitions introduced. A fire in the King's apartments in 1986 did a lot of damage to the Palace and necessitated a restoration programme which took six years to complete and was of a similar scale to that which had been undertaken in the 1880s. The apartments were re-opened by Queen Elizabeth II in 1992, and all work on the Palace was finally completed in 1995.

Harrods

Knightsbridge is centrally located in the city of Westminster, and is the indisputable epitome of opulence, refinement and class, the heart of London's social elite. Consequentially, status is bestowed upon the businesses which trade within this privileged locality, and the department store Harrods revels in its unparalleled status as London's most prestigious shopping venue.

Harrods was established as a family business in 1849 when Charles Henry Harrod, a wholesale tea merchant by trade, bought and re-named the store on Brompton Road which he had previously been renting. At this time, Harrod's business was a modest grocery store which employed two members of staff, and had a turnover of approximately £20 per week.

In 1851, the Knightsbridge area underwent a complete transformation. In preparation for the Great Exhibition, the area was enhanced by the erection of vast museums and new buildings. What had once been considered a working-class slum district quickly emerged as one of the most fashionable and affluent regions of the city.

Harrod began to expand his business, and the range of goods which he supplied widened. His profits increased, and he used this money to buy neighbouring businesses.

In 1860, Harrod sold the business to his son, Charles Digby Harrod, a 20 year old entrepreneur who began immediately to further expand the store's stock to include items such as china, glass, furniture and perfumes. His aim was to attract a slightly wealthier class of customer to the store, even providing the more eminent of them with a personalised service.

Mohamed Al Fayed, Harrods owner, serving food in the Harrods Food Hall

By 1868, Harrod was employing sixteen staff, and the turnover had increased to £1,000 per week.

When the shop was destroyed by fire in 1883, Harrod saw in the potential tragedy the opportunity to completely re-design and re-build the store. The finished store was spread over five floors all linked by a grand central staircase. Charles Digby Harrod retired in 1889, and the business was floated as a limited company. Keeping the name which had become synonymous with quality, value and style, 'Harrod's Stores Limited' was sold for £120,000.

Over the following decade, the store's new managing director, Richard Burbridge, began the process of transforming the store into the exclusive department store as we see it today. He acquired many of the neighbouring properties and land and constructed a significantly larger store. By 1902, Harrods housed 80 departments and employed almost 2,000 personnel.

Harrods remained in private ownership and continued to make frequent business acquisitions until 1959, when it was itself taken over by The House of Fraser. The group was bought for £615,000,000 by the Fayed family in 1985, but nine years later the group, with the exception of its most prestigious member, Harrods, was floated on the stock market.

Harrods's philosophy is simple: OMNIA, OMNIBUS, UBIQUE – *All things, for all people, everywhere.* In the days when communication was limited, the store's cable address was purely 'Everything, London'. From exquisite jewellery, furnishings, beauty treatments, sports equipment to dog coat fittings, aeroplanes, house construction, a Daimler ambulance service and funeral arrangements, the range of goods and services at Harrods does indeed cover almost every request imaginable. The store even supplied a baby elephant to Ronald Reagan on request. The food halls are internationally renowned and architecturally fascinating, as is the relatively recent Egyptian Hall, adorned with hieroglyphs and sphinxes.

The store now employs over 5,000 staff from over 50 different countries, and contains 330 departments on seven floors. The exterior of the building is illuminated nightly by 11,500 bulbs. On peak days, such as sales and the Christmas period, the number of customers can exceed 300,000 per day, but all those wishing to experience what Harrods has to offer must first adhere to its strict dress code, or entry will be refused.

Hever Castle

Idyllic Hever, located near Edenbridge in Kent, is a romantic double-moated castle with an extensive, sometimes tragic, history, which dates back over seven centuries to the castle's original construction in 1270. Hever is most widely known as the childhood home of Anne Boleyn, Henry VIII's ill-fated second wife.

Anne Boleyn, c.1500–1536

The construction of the Castle occurred in three phases. The first was in 1270 when the massive Gatehouse and fortified walled Bailey were built, reflecting the defensive architecture of the period. These were reached by a wooden drawbridge which crossed the surrounding moat. Two centuries later, Geoffrey Bullen acquired the Castle. Bullen had begun his career as a mercer in Norfolk, but after inheriting a large fortune, he moved to London where he became Lord Mayor and was eventually knighted.

As the castle was no longer needed for purposes of defence, Bullen's main objective was to build comfortable Tudor living apartments within the fortified walls, and it is in these that his family came to live. Sir Geoffrey's grandson, Thomas, married the Duke of Norfolk's daughter, Elizabeth, in 1498, and the couple had a son, George, and two daughters, Anne and Mary. The popular belief is that Anne was actually born in Hever Castle although there is no evidence to support this claim.

When she was old enough, Anne left England for France to serve as lady-in-waiting to the French queen. When the queen died, Anne returned to Hever whereupon her father arranged for her to become a lady-in-waiting to Henry VIII's queen, Catherine of Aragon. Anne excelled in her duties and attracted the attention of many of the noblemen at Henry's court, and indeed the attentions of the King himself. A love developed between Anne and Lord Henry Percy, but such was Henry's displeasure that the King dissolved the relationship and arranged a marriage for Lord Percy to one of the daughters of the Earl of Shrewsbury.

Anne returned to Hever, and it was here that Henry came, having originally pursued a relationship with her sister Mary, to woo her. Anne refused to become the King's mistress, and consequently Henry began to search for a way to obtain a divorce from Catherine. It was for this reason that Henry broke from the Church of Rome and established the Church of England. In 1533, Anne Boleyn (she had by now adopted the alternative spelling of her surname), married Henry VIII in Westminster Abbey.

Anne's inability to produce an heir displeased the King, and only three years after their marriage, he falsely accused her of adultery and had her executed on Tower Green.

Upon Sir Thomas's death, which followed the deaths of his wife and son, Hever Castle became the property of the Crown, and in turn it was presented to Anne of Cleves on her divorce from Henry in 1540. Anne of Cleves remained at the Castle until her death in 1557. The Castle was subsequently purchased by the Waldegraves. Sir Edward Waldegrave became the first baronet of Hever in 1642. In 1749, Hever Castle became the property of the Meade-Waldos, but it suffered from serious neglect.

Over the centuries it gradually fell into disrepair, until it was purchased in 1903 by the American millionaire William Waldorf Astor. Astor spent vast amounts of his own personal fortune on renovations to the castle, and keenly maintained historical accuracy. He built the 100 room Tudor Village, and furnished the castle's interior with beautiful antiques and artwork. He also restored the gardens, thereby creating a fairytale setting for the castle. Some of the features which he included in the gardens were the maze, the 35 acre artificial lake, dug out by local farm labourers, and the unique Italian garden, which can all be seen today.

Houses of Parliament

Edward the Confessor built the palace at Westminster in the first half of the eleventh century, and his court was subsequently held there. In 1256, Henry III moved the Great Parliament to the Palace, and for more than seven centuries since, the Palace of Westminster has been home to the English Parliament.

The Palace of Westminster, or Houses of Parliament as the buildings are more commonly known, still stands on the site of Edward the Confessor's original Palace, but the design is of the nineteenth century. When a fire broke out in 1834, Edward's palace was gutted and the only structures which could be saved were the Crypt Chapel, Westminster Hall and the cloisters.

In the wake of this devastation, a competition was launched to find the best design for a replace-ment building. Of 97 entries,

Oliver Cromwell's statue outside the House of Commons

the design submitted by architect Charles Barry and interior designer Augustus Pugin was selected. Their plans were for a magnificent palace in the Victorian Gothic revival style, with an interior which balanced large, spacious chambers with elaborate ornamentation, and combined splendid displays of wealth with the functional necessities, corridors and offices, of a working building. The Palace was also designed to complement the nearby Westminster Abbey.

Despite William IV's offer to allow Parliament to move into Buckingham Palace, work began on Charles Barry's palace in 1840, and was not completed until 1860. The final building comprised a central hall and corridor with the House of Lords and the House of Commons to the north and south. Imposing features included the clock tower which came to be popularly known as Big Ben, the massive Victoria Tower which flies the Union Jack when Parliament is sitting, and the spire above the central hall. Specially incorporated on the request of Prince Albert was the portrayal of periods in British history, depicted in the numerous sculptures which decorate the 300 m (328 yards) façade of the palace. The only feature of Barry's design which is no longer present is the stone chosen for the building. The original stone was not sufficiently durable to withstand London's atmosphere, and has gradually been replaced by a harder wearing type.

The central hall, which measures 73 m (240 ft) by 18 m (60 ft), is considered to be one of the most magnificent medieval halls in Europe and was the highest court of law in the land, and the venue for coronation banquets, until the nineteenth century. Steeped in history, it was here that the traitor Guy Fawkes was tried for his attempt to blow up the House of Lords on November 5, 1605. Outside the hall stands the statue of Oliver Cromwell who was sworn in as Lord Protector in 1653.

Barry's design for the House of Commons (the elected members of Parliament) was, as far as possible, a replica of St. Stephen's Chapel, the old meeting place for the Commons. His work however, was to stand for less than a century, destroyed by a bomb in World War II. When the House was rebuilt in 1950, the same design was followed. The members of the cabinet and the opposition face each other to conduct their discussions. As a measure to keep these discussions as orderly as possible, a distance between the two facing front benches has been marked on the floor in red lines. This distance is exactly two sword lengths and one pace apart, and members are pro-hibited from crossing this mark, hence the expression 'to toe the line'. The Table of the House is located in the centre of the chamber, and the mace is placed upon it at the start of each session. At the end of the chamber the speaker keeps order over the proceedings.

A much grander affair is the House of Lords (unelected senior members of state and church), adorned with scarlet and gold. The Queen sits on the gold throne under a regal canopy to open Parliament each November, and the Chancellor sits opposite her. Based on a tradition dating back to the time when wool was England's largest export, the Chancellor's seat is the Woolsack, a large scarlet cushion packed with wool.

Kensington Palace

Kensington Palace has been the residence of some of the most famous Kings and Queens in British history. It was the centre of the life and government of the country in the seventeenth and eighteenth centuries, was the birthplace and childhood home of Queen Victoria, and the final residence of the late Princess Diana, who stayed in the apartments in the north-west section of the palace.

Originally Nottingham House, the Jacobean Mansion was bought by William III from the Earl of Nottingham in 1689. Due to his dislike of London and his residence there at Whitehall, William was eager to move into the house at Kensington as soon as possible. Thus, rather than rebuild the property, William instead commissioned Sir Christopher Wren to make the alterations and additions necessary to transform the house into a royal residence. Wren's improvements included the addition of pavilions at the four corners of the house, the construction of the King and Queen's Royal Apartments, the Chapel Royal, a council chamber and the Great Stairs. From the Palace to Hyde Park, a road was laid down which was wide enough to carry three carriages abreast.

Mary continued improvements in the following year when William was away on campaign, and in 1891, a fire in the southern range of the Great Court necessitated further renovations.

Following the death of William in 1702, Queen Anne succeeded to the throne. With the exception of the addition of a number of new rooms, and the necessary repairs, very few changes were made to the Palace during her occupancy. She did however, lavishly furnish the property, and a substantial amount of furniture was installed by her.

When George I became King he commissioned a survey of the house, which proved it to be in a very bad state of neglect. Several proposals for dramatic rebuilding were suggested, but the King chose a more modest, yet extensive, redesign, to be carried out by Wren's replacement, William Benson, in 1718.

The restoration to the building was so protracted that during George I's reign, the state use of the palace was extremely infrequent. To George, who disliked the pomp and formality of court life, this was a welcome inconvenience, and he preferred to pass his time in the private apartments.

George II continued to use Kensington as one of his principal residences, but his death in 1760 marked the end of the palace's

Statue of Queen Victoria in Kensington Palace Gardens

use as the residence of a reigning monarch.

The Palace was uninhabited until 1798, when Edward, Duke of Kent, George III's fourth son, expressed his desire to occupy the two floors of rooms beneath the State apartments. Formerly the king's private apartments, and untouched for almost 40 years, these rooms were in quite a state of disrepair. The Duke persisted however, and the lower floors of the palace were completely converted.

When the Duke's sister, Princess Charlotte, died unexpectedly in 1817, George III found himself with no young heir to the throne. None of his twelve descendants had legitimate children to inherit his crown. The Duke consequently married Victoria, Dowager Princess of Leiningen, and their first child, Princess Victoria, was born a year later at Kensington Palace in 1819.

The Duke of Kent, and his father George III died within days of each other only nine months after the birth of the princess, who continued to live at the Palace with her mother until her coronation in 1837. As soon as Victoria received news of William IV's death and her consequent accession, she moved into Buckingham Palace.

Apartments at Kensington Palace were allocated to members of the Royal Family infrequently over the following years, but they were largely neglected and in the nineteenth century, an initiative, strongly supported by Queen Victoria, was announced to restore the Palace as closely as possible to its former appearance during the reign of George II.

Today, Kensington is a working Royal palace, and contains the offices and London residences of a number of the Royal Family. The historic parts of the palace are open to the public, and displays include the Royal Ceremonial Dress collection.

Kew Gardens

Situated between Richmond and Kew on the banks of the River Thames, are the Royal Botanic Gardens, commonly known as Kew Gardens. The area covers over 120 hectares, and comprise features such as an extensive arboretum, massive botanical greenhouses, historic buildings and elaborate water features. The Gardens' connection with royalty dates back over two centuries when the land and properties at Kew were owned by members of the Royal Family. The adjacent areas of land, the Richmond Estate and the Kew Estate, were owned by two separate branches of royalty, and were eventually joined to form one single plot.

Kew Gardens Pagoda

The Kew Estate first became the property of royalty when it was leased by Frederick, Prince of Wales, from the Capel family in 1730. Frederick participated in the laying out of the Gardens but it was after his death that his widow, Augusta, and son, George III, made the major developments at Kew. They were advised by the head gardener, William Aiton, and a botanical adviser, Lord Bute. The buildings in the Garden and grounds were designed by the architect Sir William Chambers. He decorated the estate with very fashionable pavilions and temples.

The Richmond Estate passed to George III on the death of his grandfather in 1760. In 1766, he employed 'Capability' Brown to redesign the grounds. On the death of his mother in 1772, George also inherited the neighbouring Kew Estate. Under the direction of Sir Joseph Banks, the Gardens' fame increased, notably as a result of his systematic acquisition of plants from all over the world, the interest in which ranged from economic to scientific to horticultural.

When George III and Sir Joseph Banks died in 1820, little attention was paid to the Gardens, and they consequently became a national property in 1840, upon which royal interest was renewed, and donations of additional surrounding land were offered by the Royal Family. The first official director, Sir William

Hooker, was appointed in the following year. He was responsible for the founding of the Museums of Economic Botany in 1847, and the Herbarium and Library in 1852. Decimus Burton designed the Palm House, finished in 1848, and his work on the Temperate House began in 1860.

Work passed on to Sir Joseph Hooker when his father died, and he established the Jodrell Laboratory in 1876. The Marianne North Gallery was donated to the Gardens in 1882, and on the occasion of Queen Victoria's Diamond Jubilee in 1897, the monarch presented the Gardens with Queen Charlotte's Cottage and its surrounding grounds.

It was in 1904 that the Gardens extended to their current size of 120 hectares, with the gift of the Cambridge Cottage and its garden by Edward VII to commemorate the last Duke of Cambridge.

More recent constructions include the Evolution House, the Princess of Wales Conservatory, the Sir Joseph Banks Building and the Victoria Gate Visitor Centre.

Primarily a scientific institution, the Royal Botanic Gardens' main objective is to increase the knowledge and understanding of the plant and fungal kingdoms which form the basis of life on earth. The Gardens are involved in the conservation of threatened plants, research into the use of plants to solve environmental problems on a global scale, and the education of not only scientists and horticulturalists, but also the general public, through the maintenance and development of their world-class collections.

Kew Gardens lake and research centre

Lake District National Park

The Lake District National Park, in the county of Cumbria in the North West of England, is a beautiful blend of moors, mountains, forests and lakes. Even on the dullest of days, of which the Cumbrian climate ensures there are many, the scenic splendour of the landscapes cannot fail to impress. Of the eleven National Parks within England and Wales, the Lake District is the largest. It covers an area of 2,292 km² (84 miles²).

The Neolithic stone circle of Castlerigg in the Lake District

Much of the scenery is the work of Ice Age glaciers, which scooped out the deep rock basins now occupied by Ullswater, Wast Water and the other lakes which give the region its name. Man has also, over time, contributed to its development. The history of man's influence on the Lake District can be traced back to over 5,000 years ago, at a time when the majority of Great Britain was covered in woodland. The first settlers, the Stone Age people, arrived in the area and quarried stone for axes in Great Langdale; with these they began to clear the woodland on the low ground in preparation for settlement and agriculture. As a result of the various activities undertaken in the different areas of the region, a patchwork of habitats developed which have remained to the present day.

In the late Neolithic and early Bronze Age, a large number of stone circles were constructed in the area, notably Castlerigg near Keswick. The function of the stones, which vary in size and shape, is not clear, although it is likely that they were used mainly as markers of sky burial sites or meeting places, possibly for axe traders. Some evidence suggests that they may also have been used as crude calendars, to mark special landmark festivals such as midsummer and midwinter.

There is much evidence in Cumbria of the devices used by the Romans to protect their conquests in the North of England. The Roman roads and forts which were established in the Lakeland hills are still visible, and the greatest example of this is the remarkable Hadrian's Wall. It appears unlikely that the Romans ever settled in this mountainous area, rather they used it to protect their borders, although remains of bathhouses have been found at Hardknott and Ravenglass. The name Cumbria was undoubtedly bestowed upon the region by the Celts who arrived in the area after the departure of the Romans. The Celts came to the Lakeland from Wales, and Cumberland originates from Cymru.

There was no prolific activity in the Lake District until the tenth century, when the Norse invaders settled in the valleys and lowlands. Here they cleared woodland and glacial debris, built villages, and introduced livestock to the area. The region as we see it today is largely the work of this people, and the place names and descriptions which they gave to the valleys (dales), hills (fells), clearings (thwaites) and lakes (tarns) are commonly used.

After this period, the area remained as the Norse people had designed it, although the constant dispute in the Middle Ages regarding the rightful ownership, be it English or Scottish, of the border area of Lakeland resulted in the construction of many 'pele' towers which are still present.

Following the upheaval reigned on monastic lands during Henry VIII's rule, farming families began to emerge in the Lake District. These farmers, or yeomen, had acquired wealth through the sale of timber, wool and livestock, and began to divide up the area, marking their own properties with stone walls, and by constructing farmhouses.

In the eighteenth and nineteenth centuries, the area gained recognition as an elite tourist location, probably encouraged by the works of the great English Romantic poet, William Wordsworth who was born, and had grown up, in the area, and who extolled its virtues in his work. The introduction of railways in the nineteenth century made the area accessible to the working classes, much to the displeasure of the richer tourists, and Wordsworth himself. The benefits to the local economy however, soon quietened local protests. In the twentieth century the Lake District was granted National Park status, and therein the promise of the preservation and protection of the beauty of the region. Although tourism is now a vital component of the economy of the Lake District, the effect of the 12,000,000 annual tourists is closely observed by a conscientious warden.

Lake Windermere

Now the name of the town which has grown up around it, Windermere originally referred only to the lake, the largest in England, which is centrally located in the Lake District National Park. The town of Bowness was the original village on the banks of the lake, but it has now merged with the later developed town of Windermere, and the two places are commonly referred to as one.

Named after one of the chiefs of the Viking invaders who came to the area in the tenth century, the lake, Vinander's Mere (which gradually became Windermere over centuries of mispronunciation), is 17 km (11 miles) long, 4 km (2.5 miles) wide, 60 m (200 ft) deep, and surrounded by spectacular scenery. A classic ribbon lake, it occupies a long trench eroded by a glacier. When the Lake District became popular with tourists in the eighteenth and nineteenth centuries, the number of visitors to the lake and the surrounding villages slowly began to increase. With the installation of the railway line to the lake in 1847, the fortunes of the area were changed forever.

The inhabitants of the two small villages of Bowness and Windermere (then Birthwaite) were immediately presented with new opportunities for trade and employment, and the region became a prime residential area. Large hotels and private residences were built, and local industrialists who had profited from the Industrial Revolution decided to take up residence in the area. A place formerly of little importance became a veritable hive of activity, boasting fine hotels, prestigious properties, shops and restaurants.

Today, Lake Windermere is still the most visited of the lakes in the Lake District. Some tranquil and some bustling, the towns and villages which surround the lake are able to offer a choice of atmospheres to a variety of visitors. In the midst of some of the finest scenery which England has to offer, the setting is perfect for long walks, horse-riding, climbing, cycling and paragliding, or activities on the lake itself, including boat hire, water-skiing, sailing, fishing and swimming.

Beatrix Potter and William Heelis on their wedding day

A frequent visitor to the area in the second half of the nineteenth century was the young Beatrix Potter, who had been born in London, but whose parents enjoyed the repose offered by the Lake District. One area in which the family often holidayed was Wray Castle, on the west shore of Windermere. The stories which Beatrix went on to write were inspired by the time she had spent in the Lake District, and consequently, with the royalties from her early books, she bought Hill Top Farm, a property there near Sawrey, in 1905. Tom Kitten, Jemima Puddleduck, and Samuel Whiskers are just three of the thirteen characters she wrote about or animated during her stays there.

As Beatrix earned more money from her writing, she found herself in a position to extend her property and consulted a local solicitor, William Heelis, for advice. A shared love for the Lake District united the couple, and when William proposed to Beatrix in 1912, she accepted. They were married in 1913 and made their home in Castle Cottage in Sawrey.

When Beatrix Potter died in 1943, she left 4,000 acres of land, including farms and properties, to the National Trust in order to ensure that the beauty of the land which had brought her so much happiness would be preserved for future generations.

Leisure boats moored at Ambleside on Lake Windermere

Land's End

Land's End lies at the extreme south-western tip of the county of Cornwall and, as its name suggests, is the most westerly point on the English mainland. The coastline of granite cliffs here is spectacular, and the magical air which rests over Land's End has given rise to a number of local legends of lost cities and Arthurian myths. The strongly weathered granite cliffs have probably not retreated for tens of thousands of years; this is one of the most ancient landmarks in Britain, unchanging but for the rising and falling sea.

Looking out across the Atlantic Ocean from Land's End on a clear day, it is just possible to make out the Isles of Scilly which rest on the horizon. Closer to the shore, approximately 1.6 km (1 mile) out to sea is the Longships Lighthouse.

The magnificent cliffs, sea birds, wild flowers and powerful Atlantic Ocean no longer enjoy the eerie solitude of days gone by. In 1987, Peter de Savary, an English entrepreneur, outbid the National Trust in order to build a tourist complex at the site. The complex is a series of exhibitions and displays which feature the history and heritage of the area, and which have a strong focus on nautical history and the treachery of the sea. The complex also includes souvenir shops, restaurants, bars and photo opportunities.

The signpost at Land's End

Old Cornish folklore tells of a very different place, of the lost land of Lethowstow. It is recorded that the land once extended out to the Scilly Isles, but that a huge tidal wave rose up and flooded the 140 parishes of lush orchards and magnificent towns which covered this distance. The remains of one of the greatest towns of this lost land, the City of Lions, are said to be the Seven Stones which are visible just beyond Land's End. Local fishermen are reported to have pulled up panes of ancient glass and woodwork from the reef here, and on a stormy night, the bells of the sunken towns are believed to be heard tolling.

Arthurian legend tells a similar tale, but rather than the lost land of Lethowstow, it is the legendary kingdom of Lyonnesse which lies beneath the sea. The land of Lyonnesse belonged to the noble prince Tristan, and it was to Lyonnesse that Arthur lured the armies of Mordred. With Arthur on the westernmost point of Lyonnesse, Merlin raised a thunderous earthquake which sent the waters flooding over the land, and consequently drowned Arthur's arch enemy and his followers. The land on which Arthur stood was broken up, but remained above water and now composes the Isles of Scilly. This is the legend told by Tennyson in *Idylls of the King*:

> Then rose the King and moved his host by night,
> And ever push'd Sir Mordred, league by league,
> Back to the sunset bound of Lyonesse –
> A land of old upheaven from the abyss
> By fire, to sink into the abyss again;
> Where fragments of forgotten peoples dwelt,
> And the long mountains ended in a coast
> Of ever-shifting sand, and far away
> The phantom circle of a moaning sea.
>
> TENNYSON, *IDYLLS OF THE KING*

Britain's northernmost extremity is the town of John O'Groats on the north-east tip of Scotland, and the distance between here and Land's End has been covered by numerous fundraisers and record-breakers in a variety of ways. The first recorded undertaking of the walk was by Eliuh Burritt, who completed the 1,427 km (886.3 mile) distance in 'several weeks' in 1875. Today the record stands as twelve days, three hours and forty-five minutes. Less conventionally, the distance has been covered in a wheelbarrow in 30 days, on roller skates in 9.5 days, and run backwards in 26 days and seven hours.

A slightly shorter walk, although still the longest continuous footpath in Britain is the Cornish Coastal Footpath, of which the Northern and Southern sections meet at Land's End. The walk is over 804 km (500 miles), and some of its most breathtaking scenery is found on the coastline of Land's End.

Leeds Castle

The potentially confusingly named Leeds Castle is situated in Kent, just east of Maidstone, and is named after its first owner, Leed or Ledian, the Chief Minister of Ethelbert IV, the King of Kent. By those affiliated to it, the castle is heralded as 'the loveliest castle in the world', and certainly it is a beautiful building in spectacular surroundings. As if from a fairy tale, it stands serenely on two small islands in a shimmering lake and looks out over the wooded hills which roll before it.

Originally, the property was a manor which belonged to the Saxon royal family in the ninth century. Ownership however, changed frequently over the following century as the castle was besieged and was the scene of many battles. The Saxon castle, featured in the Domesday Book of 1085, was an earthwork stronghold with wooden palisades.

Following the Norman invasion, the barons deemed it necessary to transform the structure into a strong fortress, capable of withstanding attacks from the hostile local English population. In 1119 therefore, the construction of a stone castle was commenced by Robert Crevecoeur. Today, all that remains of this castle is the cellar, beneath the late Georgian house of 1822. The cellar used to lead to the Great Hall, on the site of which now stands the Heraldry Room.

Edward I took possession of the castle in 1278, and made many alterations to it. He extended the castle, and rebuilt much of it. Around the perimeter of the larger island he built an outer wall, at the south east of which he constructed two towers and a water gate. It was during Edward's reign that the Barbican was constructed. This is rendered unique by its composition of three parts, each comprising its own entrance – drawbridge, gateway and portcullis. The outer defences were also increased by the fortification of a mill which already existed on the site. This was

an important defence mechanism, and enabled the occupants to flood the river valley through an aqueduct in the basement. The medieval keep, or Gloriette as it was known, was also built by Edward I. This however, fell into ruins in the seventeenth century when Dutch and French prisoners being held there set fire to the structure. The last siege held at the castle was in 1321, when it was eventually taken by the troops of Edward II.

The castle was transformed from a fortress to a royal residence by the most well known of all its owners, Henry VIII, in the sixteenth century. He invested a lot of money in the castle, enlarging and refurbishing it. Fearful of invasion from France and Spain however, he did retain the castle's defences.

The castle passed from royal ownership to Sir Anthony St Ledger, the Lord Deputy of Ireland, by Edward VI in 1552. It then became the property of the Smyths, and then the Culpeper family in 1632, by whom it was used as a Roundhead arsenal during the Civil War. In the eighteenth century the castle passed from the Culpepers to Lord Fairfax.

In the following centuries, the castle underwent some reconstruction and repair work, and was consistently inhabited. The castle was bought by an American heiress in 1926, who commissioned an extensive restoration which spanned three decades. On her death, the Leeds Castle Foundation was established. This body was charged with the maintenance of the building and its grounds.

Today, the castle stands as a combination of manor house, medieval castle and royal palace. It is visited for its historical importance, its decoration, and for the displays which it houses. The grounds, and the special events staged within them, also attract attention.

Were it not for the fact that Llanfairpwllgwyngyll-gogerychwyrndrobwllllantysiliogogogoch is in the record books for having the longest place name in Britain, and indeed, in Europe, it is unlikely that the the tour buses would pour in to this small town on the Isle of Anglesey in the droves which they do.

The complete English translation of the name is 'St. Mary's Church in the hollow of the white hazel near a rapid whirlpool and the church of St. Tysilio of the red cave'. Originally, the name was much shorter, simply Llanfair Pwllgwyngyll, meaning 'The Mary Church by the pool near the white hazels', but it was renamed in the nineteenth century.

The motivation for the renaming of the town was purely commercial. In the 1850s, a railway was built between Chester and Holyhead, and a local committee was established and charged with the task of inventing a scheme to encourage the travellers on the trains to visit the village, and thereby generate some much needed revenue. It is believed that the idea of extending the name of the village to the 58 letter word, under which the town is officially registered today, was proposed by a cobbler from Menai Bridge. With the acceptance of this proposal, the incredible marketing plan was implemented.

The remarkable success of the plan has continued to the present day, and although there is little else to do in Llanfairpwllgwyngyllgogerychwyrndrobwllllantysiliogogogoch, tourists regularly visit the train station to buy a platform ticket or have their picture taken by the sign as a souvenir. The people who work in the tourist information office next to the station are asked on a daily basis to both pronounce, and teach the pronunciation of, the town's full name. The novelty however, has slightly worn off for the locals, who refer to the area simply as Llanfairpwll, or Llanfair P.G.

The Isle of Anglesey is situated off the north-west coast of Wales, and is a beautiful part of the country. It is near the astounding mountain range of Snowdonia, a short distance from Caernarfon and contains scenic countryside, historic castles, ancient chamber tombs, sandy beaches and a dramatic coastline. It is the largest island in Wales, covering an area of 714km² (276 miles²), and has a population of 71,000 people. Anglesey is referred to as Môn Mam Cymru, Mother of Wales, as the land is very fertile, and it is the main producer of wheat, cattle and other farm produce for the north of Wales.

The rugged coastline of Anglesey

Anglesey is separated from the mainland by the Menai Strait, but connected, since 1826, by the Menai Bridge. Built by Thomas Telford, the bridge was the first heavy-duty iron suspension bridge of its kind in the world. Before the construction of the bridge, farmers and drivers transported their stock on the ferries which regularly crossed the Strait. In the Roman period, the coast of Anglesey was the scene of the last stand of the Druids; they were massacred on the beach there in 61 AD.

Llanfairpwllgwyngyllgogerychwyrndrobwllllan-tysiliogogogoch is not the longest place name in the world. There is a town in Thailand which is almost three times as long, containing 163 letters.

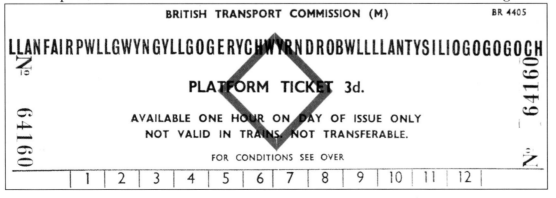

BRITISH TRANSPORT COMMISSION (M)   BR 4405

LLANFAIRPWLLGWYNGYLLGOGERYCHWYRNDROBWLLLLANTYSILIOGOGOGOCH

Nᵒ 64160

PLATFORM TICKET 3d.

AVAILABLE ONE HOUR ON DAY OF ISSUE ONLY
NOT VALID IN TRAINS. NOT TRANSFERABLE.

FOR CONDITIONS SEE OVER

64160   Nᵒ 64160

| 1 | 2 | 3 | 4 | 5 | 6 | 7 | 8 | 9 | 10 | 11 | 12 |

llantysiliogogogoch

Loch Lomond

With an enormous length of 38 km (24 miles) and a width of 8 km (5 miles), Loch Lomond is the largest freshwater lake in the United Kingdom. The loch itself is a classic ribbon lake, dammed by a terminal moraine, in turn built by a melting glacier in 9000 BC. Its famous islands are the hard areas of rock which were not slowly eroded with the rest of the valley. The loch is crossed by the Highland line, and this perhaps explains the gradual changes in the characteristics of the scenery as it moves from north to south. Loch Lomond has a remarkable beauty, a fascinating history, and a mystical presence.

The earliest inhabitants of Loch Lomond were believed to have arrived in the area during the New Stone Age in 3500BC. These people became known as the Caledonii tribes, or 'people of the woods', and their existence is verified by the stone circles and burial cairns which can be located in the area. A slightly better quality of life is indicated by studies of the settlements which were constructed in the area during the Iron Age.

When the Romans invaded Britain in the first century, they advanced towards Scotland, and the Caledonii tribes were forced northwards. When the Romans departed in the third century, three ancient kingdoms rose up around the loch. These were the kingdoms of Strathclyde to the south, Dalriada, kingdom of the celts, to the north west, and Pictland to the north-east.

Christianity was brought to the area by the Irish missionaries in the sixth and seventh centuries. The early Christians regarded Loch Lomond as a place of sacred pilgrimage, and some of the 37 islands in the loch provided ideal retreats and bases for the construction of priories and churches. The island of Inchmurrin is the largest island in the loch, and named after St. Mirrin who spent a considerable amount of time there.

Viking invaders attacked Dumbarton, the capital of Strathclyde, in the ninth century and destroyed the religious settlements. According to Irish legend, they took thousands of prisoners, and stole the riches of the region. With the capture of Dumbarton, the British dynasty in Strathclyde declined and was slowly absorbed into the developing Scottish kingdom.

Following the Norman invasion in the twelfth century, the Earldom of Lennox, which encompassed Loch Lomond and all of modern Dumbartonshire, was created. The Earls of Lennox were powerful, and gave land to the families in their favour. On the west side, land was gifted to the MacFarlanes and Colquhouns, and on the east side, it was granted to the Buchanans and Grahams. The times however, were not peaceful, and there were constant battles for land and livestock. The power struggle between the clans culminated in 1603 with the massacre of the Colquhouns by the MacGregors. The MacGregor chief was consequently executed, and protection or harbouring of any of their clan became an offence. The most famous outlaw of the MacGregor clan was Rob Roy.

Loch Lomond has been attracting tourists to the area for centuries, and its visitors have included celebrated authors, poets, statesmen, kings and queens.

Loch Lomond has a unique place in Scottish folklore and is surrounded by a number of myths and mysteries. One of the legends of Loch Lomond is transcribed in the famous song, written, it is believed, at the time of the failed Jacobite rising of 1745. The song is the story of two of Bonnie Prince Charlie's men, captured in Carlisle. One was to be executed, and the other set free. Written by the prisoner facing death, the song describes the different routes which were to be taken by the two men on their return to Scotland. The spirit of the doomed man would take the low road, whereas his saved comrade would have to struggle over the longer, more treacherous road of the rugged country.

O ye'll tak' the high road and I'll tak' the low road,
An' I'll be in Scotland afore ye;
But me and my true love will never meet again
On the bonnie, bonnie banks O' Loch Lomond

Loch Ness

Loch Ness may not be the largest of the lakes in Scotland, or the United Kingdom, but it is an area of truly outstanding natural beauty. Its global recognition however, comes not from its scenic surroundings or picturesque location in the north of Scotland, but results from the tales, reported sightings and photographic evidence of the 'monster' which lurks beneath its waters.

Were a monster to exist, Loch Ness would be the perfect place for it to hide. The loch was formed by the Great Glen, and is one of a chain of lakes, rivers and canals which link the North Sea with the Atlantic Ocean. Loch Ness covers a distance of approximately 37 km (23 miles), from Fort Augustus to Inverness,

Sunday Mail Front Page, November 23, 1975

and its average depth is 137 m (450 ft), although this drops to nearly 304 m (1,000 ft) in places, and contains underwater caves. It is deep and dark, with strong currents and bitterly cold waters.

Details of a monster were first recorded in the sixth century, when St. Colomba was reputed to have saved a swimmer in the loch from the jaws of an unidentified monster. Rumours about the creature's existence were infrequently circulated in the centuries which followed, but it was only with the completion of the A82 road along the side of the loch in 1933 that the recorded sightings of the affectionately named 'Nessie' soared, and the mystery

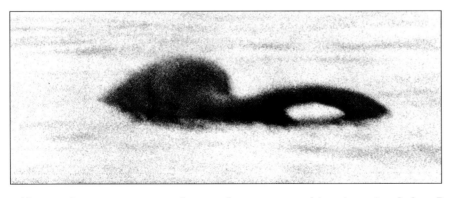

'I saw the nearest approach to a dragon or pre-historic animal that I have ever seen in my life. It crossed my road about fifty yards ahead and appeared to be carrying a small lamb or animal of some kind.'

– LETTER FROM MR SPICER TO THE *INVERNESS COURIER*, FOLLOWING HIS SIGHTING ON JULY 22, 1933.

developed into the phenomenon of the present day. Most of the reports described an enormous animal with a long, tapering neck, a small head and a huge body, sometimes with a hump on its back. The creature was sighted both in the loch and on land.

The first photographic evidence of the Loch Ness monster was presented by Hugh Gray in 1933, but more famous was the photograph taken by Colonel Robert Wilson in 1934. This created huge excitement amongst those who believed that it was conclusive proof of the evidence of the monster. It caused an even greater commotion when, almost 60 years later, Christian Spurling confessed that he had helped to make the model monster in the photograph, and revealed the 'evidence' to be fake.

Efforts to find Nessie have been exhaustive, and have included underwater cameras, scanning sonars, giant nets, echo sounders and even submarines. Amateurs and professionals alike arrive at the shores of Loch Ness hoping to be the first to gather the definitive proof of the existence of the elusive creature. None however, have been successful.

From the reported sightings, a description of Nessie has emerged which links her in appearance to the Plesiosaurus, an aquatic species of dinosaur, extinct for over 65,000,000 years. Suggestions have also been made that the monster could be a large mammal, such as a primitive whale, or long-necked otter or seal. Were this the case however, she would be expected to emerge from the water more frequently and therefore be sighted more often. The basin beneath the waters of the loch was, in any case, filled to the brim with ice until 10,000 years ago, so a prehistoric dinosaur could not have survived in it.

There is also debate regarding the impossibility of just one Loch Ness Monster. Marine biologists estimate the minimum number of a single species required to maintain its existence would be fourteen. There have been no sightings of a group of Loch Ness Monsters.

Nessie is an image inextricably linked with Scotland. She features regularly in magazine articles, documentaries, and has even had film roles. She is used in advertising, and generates a more than healthy revenue for the Scottish Tourist Board. It is estimated that the bookmaker William Hill would owe over £1,000,000 if Nessie's existence were ever to be conclusively proved.

London Eye

In the summer of 1999, one of the most famous skylines in the world welcomed a new structure which now stands proudly as the fourth tallest construction in London, and a symbol of the new millennium and beyond. The London Eye, or Millennium Wheel, was conceived and designed by the London architects Julia Barfield and David Marks, and is a privately funded venture between them, British Airways and the Tussauds Group.

The London Eye was designed to embrace the new millennium, and the concept of a wheel was proposed as a symbol of the cycle of life and the turning of time. The wheel both commemorates London's history and anticipates its future. Although a landmark in its own right, the London Eye was designed to be more than just a monument. It is an attraction which enables its visitors to observe the city of London from an entirely new perspective.

One of the London Eye's 32 passenger capsules

Due to the immense size of the structure, and the impossibility of its manufacture at one single site, work on the many different components of the London Eye was carried out throughout Europe. British Steel provided the material for the main structure which was constructed in Holland. Czech engineers cast the hub and spindle, the bearings were manufactured in Germany, the cables made in Italy, and the 32 passenger-carrying capsules were constructed in France. All the completed individual parts were then transported to London, where they were sailed up the River Thames on a barge to the site of assembly. At 330 tonnes, the hub and spindle was the heaviest piece of the London Eye, and consequently, care had to be taken to ensure that the platforms which had been laid down at the site could in fact bear the weight. These temporary platforms had been built up from the river bed, and it was on these that the London Eye was horizontally assembled.

Once fully compiled, the London Eye measured a record-breaking 135 m (442 ft) in diameter, the biggest observation wheel in existence, and weighed an enormous 1,900 tonnes. The foundations of the legs were laid in the Jubilee Gardens, and the legs themselves were hinged to enable the smooth elevation of the wheel from its horizontal to its vertical position. It was not until the structure was firmly in place that the passenger capsules were fitted to the rim of the wheel. Equipment used to assemble the London Eye included one of Europe's largest floating cranes, capable of lifting 800 tonnes.

The capsules were designed specifically to offer their passengers an all-encompassing view of London. From whichever angle the city is observed, the field of vision is clear and unobstructed, as extreme care was taken in the design to ensure that no part of the structure interfered with the passengers' view. A complete 360 degree rotation of the wheel lasts 30 minutes, and the capsules can accommodate 25 people in each. The London Eye therefore boasts the capacity to manage a phenomenal 1,600 visitors per hour. On a clear day, the viewing range from the capsules extends over 40 km (25 miles), enabling the visitor to see as far as Windsor Castle.

Long Man of Wilmington

Little is known about the mysterious Long Man, custodian of the village of Wilmington in East Sussex. Whether he is a symbol of fertility, the representation of an ancient warrior, or without meaning at all and merely an impulsive creation, has been debated by archaeologists and historians over many centuries. With no conclusive proof however, the myths cannot be dispelled nor the truth revealed.

The facts are that the Long Man is 68 m (226 ft) high, and his home is the slope of Windover Hill. The earliest reference to him is a drawing, discovered only at the end of the twentieth century, by the surveyor John Rowley in 1710. Rowley's drawing displays marked differences between the figure in the early eighteenth century and the figure as we see it today. It appears from the drawing that facial features were clearly visible, the head was in the shape of a helmet, and the feet were pointing in a different direction. That the outline of the Long Man has also changed is confirmed by Rowley. The shape of the figure was originally created by mere indentations into the grass, rather than a clear solid line which, until the nineteenth century rendered the Long Man invisible in certain conditions. In 1874 however, it is recorded that the position of the figure was marked with yellow bricks. These bricks did not follow the original outline, but were approved of by the Duke of Devonshire and the Sussex Archaeological Society. The legs, which should be splayed, have never been corrected.

In 1891, the yellow bricks were replaced with white bricks, although these were painted green for the duration of the Second World War in order not to serve as a convenient landmark for enemy planes. With the conclusion of the war, the bricks were repainted white. The outline was again slightly altered in 1969 when 770 concrete blocks replaced the bricks.

Theories abound regarding the origins and history of the Long Man of Wilmington. Some believe that the figure is a representation of a Roman standard bearer, a similar shape having been carved on to Roman coins. Another similar figure, although helmeted as in Rowley's drawing, can be found on ornaments created in Anglo-Saxon times. Others believe that he did not come into existence until many centuries later, and was purely the elaborate artwork of a creative monk from the nearby priory. His creation has also been ascribed to the monks for various other reasons, the main ones being simply that they were heretical, members of the Occult, or innocently portraying the image of a pilgrim. Although less obviously sexual than the giant at Cerne Abbas, the Long Man has also been regarded as a fertility symbol or idol. Another suggestion is that he is the guardian of a gateway, the poles which he is holding being in fact an entrance, either to heaven or to the underworld.

Windover Hill was a focus of activity in prehistory, from 3500 BC until the Iron Age. The Long Man is likely to belong to this period. The intended viewing point, the churchyard, was planted with a yellow tree in 400, well before the arrival of Christian missionaries. The church blocks the ancient sight-line, probably deliberately.

The site is also infrequently used for Pagan rituals. Offerings have been found on the image, and during the Gulf War, a Wiccan priest came to the hill to counter the power of Saddam Hussein.

The maintenance of the Long Man is now carried out by the South Downs Conservation Board. The repainting is carried out annually, and involves the removal of overgrowing grass, and the application of two fresh coats of paint. The site of the Long Man is officially owned by the Sussex Archaeological Society, and has been since 1925 when it was given to the then Sussex Archaeological Trust by the Duke of Devonshire.

The ruins of Wilmington Priory

Marble Arch

Marble Arch, like many of London's most famous landmarks, was the work of the architect John Nash. His original design for the Arch, inspired by the triumphal Constantine Arch in Rome, was as a grand gateway to Buckingham Palace, a transformation of Buckingham House which he had been commissioned to design in 1826 by George IV. This gateway was to be the palace's main entrance, and solely for royal use.

In order to make room for this imposing entrance to the palace, the north and south wings of Buckingham House were removed and demolished. They were rebuilt on a much grander scale with the Arch as the centrepiece of the enlarged courtyard.

The Arch was constructed of white carrara marble, which in the nineteenth century cost around £80,000. Corinthian columns stand between its three archways, sculptural reliefs in the spandrels, and wreaths at the ends. Edward Hodges Bailey designed the spandrels of the south side, and these portray winged Victories, the main reliefs depict a naval warrior, the panels to either side displaying Justice, and Peace and Plenty. Richard Westmacott designed the female figures of the north side. These figures represent England, Scotland and Ireland.

The palace remained as Nash, and then Edward Blore, had designed it for almost 20 years, but with the accession to the throne of Queen Victoria, and her subsequent move to Buckingham Palace with her newly married husband Prince Albert, the palace, as a residence, proved less than satisfactory. In Victoria's opinion, her new home had too few bedrooms for their guests, and she was displeased with the absence of nurseries.

The solution was to build a fourth wing, but this was not possible due to the position of the Arch. The decision was consequently taken to move the marble arch to the location where it still stands to this day, at the north-east corner of Hyde Park in the area of Tyburn. Here, it serves as a gateway between Bayswater and Marylebone.

Although Marble Arch has remained in this location since it was placed there in 1851, its surroundings have changed considerably. Numerous road improvements and alterations have left the Arch in the middle of a traffic island in one of London's busiest areas. It is nonetheless an impressive sight. The strict convention laid down in 1826 that the Arch was for the sole use of the Royal Family is still observed today, and only senior members of the Royal Family, the Royal Horse Artillery and the King's Troops are granted access to pass beneath Marble Arch.

Tyburn was regarded by some as an inappropriate location for such a palatial monument. Until 1783, Tyburn had been home to London's gallows, and it was here that the city's criminals were brought to be hanged. The 'Tyburn Tree', the permanent gallows, was the scene of very well-attended, gruesome executions.

Also in the area, the less macabre, but probably less crowd-pleasing, Speakers' Corner is on the north-eastern edge of Hyde Park. Here, a variety of topics are debated by orators and hecklers alike.

JOHN NASH
1752 — 1835
ARCHITECT

Mayflower Steps

The story of the Pilgrim Fathers is the story of a small group of devoutly religious English men and women who fled persecution in their own country to found the new World. These Puritan pioneers sailed from Plymouth Harbour on 6 September, 1620, in a ship named *The Mayflower*.

The Pilgrim Fathers had originally set sail in two boats, *The Mayflower* and *The Speedwell*, from Southampton in August 1620, but they encountered trouble off the coast of Land's End, and were forced to return to Plymouth. *The Speedwell* was deemed unseaworthy, so her passengers joined those of *The Mayflower*, which departed for Cape Cod alone the following month. On board were 102 passengers and 48 seamen.

The White Gateway to the Ocean

The wind and the waves were treacherous, sickness was prolific and food was scarce, but the Pilgrim Fathers refused to turn back. Eventually, 65 days later, the land at Cape Cod came into view. Before landing, the founding fathers anchored their ship off Princetown, where they carefully outlined the Mayflower Compact, a system of government for the colony and, it is believed, the first written constitution in the world. Therein they pledged themselves 'solemnly and mutually, in the presence of God and of one another,' to form a body politic, to frame such laws as they might need, to which they promised 'all due submission and obedience.'. They came ashore on December 21, 1620, and found a land not dissimilar to that which they had left. There they established a new colony, named Plymouth, and they formed both an amicable and respectful relationship with the native North American people.

The years which followed the Pilgrim Fathers' arrival in Plymouth were hard for the colony, and over half of *The Mayflower*'s crew did not survive their first winter. The weather conditions were harsh, and the cold winter's climate defeated many of the party. Therefore, when the founding fathers reaped their first plentiful harvest they enjoyed a Thanksgiving feast of cod, seabass and wildfowl. This Thanksgiving day is still celebrated annually as a national holiday in the United States.

For over two centuries there was no commemoration in Plymouth, England, of the place from where the pioneers had left their homes for a new life of religious liberty in the United States. In 1891 however, the descendants of the Pilgrim Fathers dedicated the Mayflower Stone to their ancestors. This was then covered in 1934 by a stone gateway, donated by the Mayor of Plymouth, and called 'The White Gateway to the Ocean'.

The Mayflower Steps are visited annually by tourists. Here, a plaque commemorates the brave men and women who boarded *The Mayflower* from this spot. It has been claimed however, that these steps do not in fact mark the spot from which the Pilgrim Fathers left for the new World as these are on reclaimed land. The original embarkation is claimed to have occurred from a nearby cliff face.

In 1957, *The Mayflower II*, a replica of the original *Mayflower*, was built as a gift to America from England. The replica ship was sailed across the Atlantic from Plymouth, England, to Plymouth, Massachusetts, where it now remains. For the first part of its life, the ship served as a museum, but in more recent years, it has been sailed, and even led the Tall Ships procession through the Cape Cod Canal.

Above: The Pilgrim Fathers preapre to set sail on the Mayflower
Right: The Mayflower II, a replica of the original ship

Menai Bridge

The Menai Strait, the narrow, 25 km (15 miles) long divide of water which separates the Isle of Anglesey from the Welsh mainland was, until 1826, only traversable by boat. It was however, a hazardous journey, and the numerous changeable currents often capsized ships, or led them to run aground, with frequently tragic results.

When the United Kingdom and Ireland were joined by the Act of Union in 1800, the number of people crossing the Strait to reach the port of Holyhead, from where the ferries departed for Ireland, dramatically increased. As a direct result, Thomas Telford began to draft plans for a bridge over the Strait which would ease the route and facilitate the access to Holyhead. The proposed plans for a bridge met with much opposition from the ferrymen who operated across the Strait, but nevertheless construction of Telford's bridge began in 1819.

Thomas Telford was the chief engineer, with William Alexander Provis as the resident engineer. Several designs were drawn up, but the one chosen was that of an iron suspension bridge, the first of its kind designed to bear heavy traffic in the world. In total, the bridge is 304 m (1,000 ft) with a span of 176 m (579 ft) between

its two towers. One of the most important of the requirements for the bridge was that it should be no less than 30 m (100 ft) above the highest level of the tide. This provision was made to allow tall sailing ships to pass underneath.

The limestone for the arches and piers of the bridge was brought by boat from Penmon Quarries, and the iron came from Shrewsbury. To prevent rusting, the iron was boiled in warm linseed oil before its use on the bridge.

The stonework of the bridge was finished in 1824, but by far the most arduous task was the raising of the sixteen massive chains which were to hold up the road between the two towers. This was eventually completed in 1825, and celebrations were consequently arranged. On July 9, 1825, three workman were the first to cross the bridge, and ran its distance with a band playing the national anthem to commemorate the event. At the same time, a local cobbler sat on the chains and completed a pair of shoes.

In the following month the final stage of the work was commenced, the task of joining the roadway from the chains. When this was completed a 21-gun salute was fired, and on January 30, 1826, the bridge was officially opened. In total, the bridge had reduced the travelling time from London to Holyhead from 36 to 27 hours.

Since 1826, a number of amendments have been made to the bridge. It was strengthened to accommodate an increase in traffic at the end of the 1930s, when the road surface also necessitated repair after damage in strong winds. In 1893, the wooden deck was replaced by steel. Weight restrictions on vehicles often meant that lorries would have to carry their loads over the bridge in two trips, and sometimes bus conductors were even forced to ask some of their passengers to get off the bus and walk across to the other side. By 1940 therefore, the old iron chains had been replaced by steel ones, and the weight of individual vehicles could be increased.

With the increase in rail travel during the nineteenth century, and the decision that it would not be feasible to uncouple the carriages and draw them across the Menai Bridge using horses as originally suggested, the Britannia Bridge, designed by Robert Stephenson, was completed in 1850. Following a devastating fire in 1970, the Britannia Bridge was rebuilt, this time as a bridge on two levels, one carrying trains and the other carrying road traffic.

The re-construction of the Britannia eased the volume of traffic across the Menai Bridge, but over time the traffic flow continued to rise steadily. One suggested solution was to build a tunnel underneath the Menai Strait. This is however, potentially hazardous due to the formation of the Strait from an occasionally active geological fault.

White Knight says to Alice
'I heard him then, for I had just completed my design.
To keep the Menai Bridge from rust.
By boiling it in wine.'
– LEWIS CARROL, *THROUGH THE LOOKING GLASS*

Millennium Dome

To one man, the Prime Minister, it is a 'great British achievement'. To another, the Prince of Wales, it is a 'monstrous blancmange'. The Millennium Dome, or more accurately, the Millennium Experience, was opened on the first day of the new millennium, January 1, 2000, and was intended to be the centrepiece of the millennium celebrations and a tribute to human achievement at the dawn of a new age.

The idea for an enormous dome to mark the coming of the new millennium was originally conceived by the Conservative government in 1994, and although it was initially opposed, the idea was eventually approved by a committee of MPs in the following year. Backing for the project had reluctantly been given to the Conservatives by the Labour party, and therefore when Labour won the general election in 1997, the future of the Dome was extremely uncertain. Labour's support however, was reaffirmed in June 1997, and responsibility for the project was awarded to Peter Mandelson.

The total cost of the Dome was initially estimated at £758,000,000, a cost to be split between four sources, the main contributor being the Millennium Commission, one of the five distributors of the proceeds from the National Lottery. The operating company appointed to run the Exhibition was the New Millennium Experience Company.

The atmosphere of uncertainty surrounding the Dome proved hard to dispel, and it increasingly appeared that although the idea of the Millennium Dome was welcomed by the majority, no attention had been paid to the finer details of the project. Concerns were raised over the lack of information regarding the contents of the Dome, the necessity of revising and increasing the capacity of the transport routes to Greenwich, and what exactly was to become of the structure after it had served its sole purpose and the exhibition was closed at the end of the year 2000. Consternation was also expressed regarding the unpredictable final cost of the project.

In spite of these fears, construction began on the Millennium Dome shortly after the confirmation of Labour's continued commitment to the project in 1997. The area chosen for the Dome was the site of a former gasworks in Greenwich, south east London, and the architect commissioned was Richard Rogers, whose previous works included the globally renowned Pompidou Centre in Paris. Covering an area of 100,000 m² (119,599 yards²), with a circumference of 1 km (0.6 miles), and a height of 50 m (164 ft) at its highest point, the Millennium Experience is the world's largest covered area, estimated to cover the equivalent space of ten St. Paul's Cathedrals, or 18,000 double decker buses. Twelve 100 m (328 ft) high steel masts suspend the structure, held on a net of high strength steel cable which measures over 70 km (43 miles).

Inside, the central area of the Dome is a large open arena, designed for a single theatrical show, and around the inner edge are the restaurants and retail outlets, and the fourteen 'zones' of the exhibition. These zones cover a collection of themes, including Body, Home Planet, Journey, Self Portrait and Work, and are mostly interactive, educational and entertaining.

With the closure of the Dome 365 days after it had first opened, debate concerning the structure, which had begun and concluded as one of the UK's most controversial public projects, still raged. Even as an empty building, the Dome was costing £1,800,000 pounds per month to maintain. It is now widely believed that the Millennium Dome will be transformed into a sound-proof 20,000-seater sports and entertainment complex.

The Body Zone, one of the fourteen zones created in the Millennium Dome

Millennium Stadium

One of the most dominant sights in the capital of Wales is the Millennium Stadium, built on the site of the internationally famous Cardiff Arms Park, and widely believed to be one of the greatest rugby stadiums in the world. Shortlisted for the British Construction Industry Major Project Award 2000, the Millennium Stadium has retained the magical and glorious atmosphere of Cardiff Arms Park, but has also introduced a multitude of modern improvements. These have therefore heralded the movement of Welsh rugby into the twenty-first century.

An initial bid for funding from the Millennium Commission was unsuccessful, but a further attempt secured a grant of £46,000,000. With this awarded, the Millennium Stadium PLC was established. The Welsh Rugby Union own the freehold, but appointed a 50 year lease to the Millennium Stadium PLC and charged them with the task of managing and marketing the Stadium during this time.

On March 15, 1997, the last international match was played at Cardiff Arms Park, with the last international try for Wales scored by Rob Howley. On the following day, the deal was signed with contractors to demolish one of Wales's greatest sites and, in its place, to build another. The final match of the old ground saw a Cardiff victory over Swansea.

For the two years during which Wales had no rugby ground, their home fixtures were played at Wembley Stadium. They finally returned to Cardiff on June 26, 1999. Initially crowds were

Wales's Scott Quinnell scores a try against England in the Six Nations Rugby tournament

restricted, but on October 1, all 72,500 seats were filled by those coming to witness Wales's victory over Argentina in the incredible opening ceremony of the fourth World Cup.

The Millennium Stadium proudly boasts the first retractable roof to be fitted on any stadium in the United Kingdom. The scale of this undertaking was phenomenal. The roof holds nearly 8,000 tonnes of steel, a weight which is supported by four 93 m (305 ft) high masts. The sliding mechanism of the roof has a length of 220 m (721 ft), and a depth of 15 m (49 ft). In total, the time taken for the roof to open is 20 minutes.

When the year 2000 was rung in in Cardiff, the Millennium Stadium was, unsurprisingly, at the heart of the celebrations. The Manic Street Preachers, one of the most popular and successful of Welsh bands, played to 60,000 people in the largest indoor concert ever to be held in Europe.

Although its main focus is sport, the Stadium stages a diversity of events. These include trade shows, concerts, conferences, banquets and even wedding ceremonies.

Mount Snowdon

Within the Snowdonia National Park majestically towers the 1,085 m (3,559 ft) high Mount Snowdon, after which the park was actually named. The English name for the mountain comes from the Saxon term, Snow Dun, meaning the snow hill or fortress. Its Welsh name, Yr Widdfa, translates as 'Great Tomb' and derives from the Arthurian legend that a giant, slain by King Arthur, was laid to rest on the mountain's summit.

Mount Snowdon is the highest of the Welsh mountains, glacially eroded, with corries and arêtes all around it, and is thus perennially popular with both amateur and professional walkers, hikers and climbers alike. 500,000 people come to Snowdonia to climb the mountain per year. On a clear day, the views from the summit are spectacular, and encompass almost the entirety of North Wales. The experience is no less unique in cloudy conditions, the clouds swirl underfoot clearing occasionally to reveal the valley below.

The summit of Mount Snowdon has served as a training ground for the members of Sir Edmund Hillary's team prior to their successful expedition to conquer Mount Everest. Visitors have also included the former Prime Minister, William Gladstone, who gave a speech from a small rock, which now bears his name, on the proposed freedom for Wales and Ireland. The poet William Wordsworth recorded his experience of reaching the summit before sunrise in his work entitled *The Prelude*.

The Snowdon Mountain Railway

*...With forehead bent
Earthward, as if in opposition set
Against an enemy, I panted up
With eager pace, and no less eager
thoughts...*

One of Snowdon's less enthusiastic visitors was the Prince of Wales. On sight of the crowds, litter and the cafe at the summit, he disparagingly remarked that he had arrived at 'the highest slum in Europe'.

There are a number of routes to Snowdon's summit from the surrounding villages, and they vary in

difficulty, from energetic walks to full climbing routes. The Llanberis Path and the Snowdon Ranger Path are among the easiest. The Miner's Track, from Pen-y-Pass, is so called because it was used by the miners who needed to get to work.

A less energetic option is also available in the form of the Snowdon Mountain Railway, which runs from Llanberis to Snowdon's summit. The line is rack-and-pinion, the only one of its kind in the United Kingdom, and it was completed in 1896 as a replacement for the local guides and their mountain ponies who had been accompanying Victorian tourists to watch the sunrise from the summit for decades. In its first day of operation, Engine No.1 fell into a ravine. Although the coaches did not fall, two passengers were so frightened that they jumped, and one was killed. Despite this tragic beginning, there has not been another accident on the railway since that day.

The inhospitable nature and rugged terrain of the mountains made it a perfect refuge for Welsh revolutionaries, such as Llywelyn ap Gruffydd, the Welsh armies defying Edward I, and Owain Glyndŵr, all battling against English oppression.

As well as the impressive Mount Snowdon, Snowdonia National Park hosts a wide variety of natural delights, including forests, glacial valleys, waterfalls, rivers and moorlands. It was into one of the lakes of the park, Lyn Llydaw, that the mortally wounded King Arthur is believed to have thrown the mighty Excalibur.

Needles

Marking the westernmost point of the Isle of Wight, the Needles are the three jagged chalk rock formations which rise out of the sea. These, and the red and white banded lighthouse on the third and furthest rock, combine to form the Island's most famous landmark.

At the time of the last Ice Age, the Isle of Wight was connected to Dorset by a chalk ridge which ran westwards across the centre of the island and into the sea. At that time, the body of water between the south coast of England and this chalk ridge was the Solent river, which flowed south between Wight and Selsey to join the great Channel River. The tributaries of the Solent River, and the battering of the sea's waves from the south, gradually wore away this chalk band, eventually breaking it down completely. The Needles and the old Harry Rocks in Dorset are its last remaining sections. For a long time, the Needles consisted of four chalk pinnacles, but the fourth rock, known as 'Lot's Wife' and which was much taller and more slender than the others collapsed during a storm in 1764. The three remaining rocks rise to a height of 30 m (100 ft). The Needles and neighbouring cliffs were, at that time, frequented by swarms of sea birds, puffins, razorbills, cormorants and gulls. The local people used to abseil down the rocks to catch them for their feathers.

These hazardous rocks have always been a threat to the ships and seamen negotiating the waters of the Solent. In 1781 therefore, Trinity House was petitioned by the merchants and ships' owners who insisted upon the installation of a lighthouse. In January 1782, a patent was secured which dictated that a light should be kept burning during the night season. It was not however, until 1785 that Trinity House authorised the construction of three lighthouses, one of which was at the Needles. The lighthouse was built according to the designs of R. Jupp, formerly a surveyor for the East India Company. On September 29, 1786, the tower was illuminated.

In its location on a clifftop, 144 m (472 ft) above sea level, the light from the tower was often eclipsed by sea mists and fog, on which occasions it was effectively rendered useless to the mariners who were reliant on it. In 1859, Trinity House unveiled plans for a new lighthouse to be erected on the furthest of the three chalk rocks. This is the lighthouse which guides boats away from the rocks today.

The tower was designed by James Walker at a cost of £20,000. The circular tower is 33.25 m (109 ft) high and is constructed in granite. Its diameter is uniform, but the base is unevenly stepped in order to break the sea's waves and thus prevent them from sweeping up the tower. In 1987, a helipad was constructed on top of the lighthouse. The tower is now automated and has been so since 1994.

Directly overlooking the famous Needles is the Needles Old Battery, a Victorian coastal fort which was established in 1862 as a defence against French invasion. Due to its spectacular location, the fort was later used as a lookout during the Second World War. At the base of the cliffs are the coloured sands of Alum Bay, from where the Needles extend out to sea.

The Needles are both a navigational and a recreational landmark for yachtsmen and women from all over the world. The rocks are a focal point of the 'Round the Island Race', the prestigious, internationally-renowned yacht-racing event in which sailors compete for the Gold Roman Bowl, the trophy first presented by the founder of the race, Cyril Windeler. The race commences in Cowes, and the yachts race anti-clockwise around the island over a course of 92 km (50 nautical miles). Over 1,500 yachts participate, professionals and amateurs compete side by side.

Yachts competing in the Round the Island Race

Old Man of Hoy

Of the islands in the Orkney group, Hoy, from the Norse term Haey meaning 'high island', is the second largest. The island measures 147 km² (57 miles²) in area, and the landscape varies quite noticeably from the north to the south. The terrain of the northwest area is hilly and characteristic of the Highlands, whereas the south and east are more fertile and low-lying. As its name suggests, Hoy hosts some of the highest vertical cliffs in Britain. The highest point on Hoy, and on Orkney, is the 479 m (1,571 ft) high summit of Ward Hill, from which it is possible to view almost all of the islands in the Orkney group. Hoy's most famous landmark however, is the 137 m (450 ft) sandstone sea stack which is known as The Old Man of Hoy.

The Old Man of Hoy rises dramatically from the Atlantic and lies to the north of Rora Head. It is made of old red sandstone with a basalt base, separated from the coast by the combined erosive forces of the sea and the wind. These powers of nature are still having an effect on the rock and it is debatable as to how

much longer the Old Man of Hoy can withstand the constant lashings of wind and wave before it succumbs to the elements and crashes into the sea.

The Old Man of Hoy is, as a natural phenomenon, a marvel to behold, but its fame lies mainly within the climbing fraternity, and it is renowned for the challenge which it presents to the most accomplished of climbers. The first successful ascent of the Old Man of Hoy was made by Sir Christopher Bonington in 1966, a televised event which consequently thrust Hoy into the spotlight, and made it a compulsory destination for those who dared to attempt the climb. With the advances in technology and equipment over the years, the ascent has now been made accessible to less-experienced climbers and the challenge has consequently been completed on many occasions.

Although famed primarily for its 'Old Man', and for the climbing opportunities which it presents, Hoy boasts a wide variety of attractions and activities. Evidence of a rich history is littered across the island, with sites dating back to prehistoric times and the Vikings. Hoy contains the only rock-cut chambered tomb in Britain. The tomb, the Dwarfie Stane, dates from around 3000 BC and is a large block of sandstone which stands alone beneath the Dwarfie Hamars. A square hole in the side marks the entrance, and a short passage leads to two small chambers on either side. A large block of sandstone was used to seal the opening, and on both the inside and outside, Victorian graffiti is evident.

The island of Hoy also played an important role in Britain's naval history. The Martello Towers on either side of Longhope Bay were constructed between 1813 and 1815, and were designed to protect the Baltic Conveys from the American Privateers while they waited for naval escort during the Napoleonic Wars. The Lyness Naval Base and Interpretation Centre is the only remaining evidence of the large World War II naval base on the island.

Equally rich in natural history and geology, Hoy is home to a number of northern plant communities normally associated with mountain areas. These are to be seen in a natural setting which is seldom rivalled in Britain. The island is beautifully rugged in parts, and offers spectacular walks along the hills and sea cliffs. One of the most stunning areas on Hoy is Rackwick Bay, surrounded by high red sandstone cliffs and heather laden hills. The journey to the beach is across a mass of red and yellow banded boulders, moulded into smooth spheres by the breaking waves of the Atlantic. Here, composer Sir Peter Maxwell Davies lives and writes his music.

Peak District National Park

The utopian landscape of the Peak District, in the very heart of Britain, is of such a spectacular beauty that it was the first area in Britain to be designated a National Park, a status it has held since 1951. The Peak District is principally in Derbyshire, although its 1,437 km² (555 miles²) of open countryside spill over into five neighbouring counties. Surrounded by urban and industrial towns, the Peak District is completely unspoilt and has remained a haven of natural beauty, of woodland, rivers and moors.

There is clear evidence that the countryside of the Peak District has been appreciated by man for thousands of years. Flint blades from Mesolithic hunters, the Bronze Age stone circle on Stanton Moor, and the hill forts constructed by the settlers in the Iron Age all testify to the Peak District's enduring appeal. The Romans were also attracted to the area, and were followed by the Saxons, Danes and Normans, all of whom built up their own farms and villages on the land. By 1086, the Domesday Book records that the area contained a number of hamlets, and that a large section of the land had been allocated as a Royal Forest, specifically designated as a hunting ground for the king and his company.

Throughout medieval times, small farming communities began to prevail in the Peak District. It was also around this time that the first visitors started to arrive in the area, mostly traders traversing the moors between the important trading centres. The Industrial Revolution gave rise to an increase in tourism as people were desperate to escape the grime and dirt of the towns and consequently sought refuge in the clean air of the Peak District's countryside.

Tourism rapidly increased, and consequently the demand grew for more freedom of movement across the Peak District. Much of the land was privately owned and therefore many visitors were denied access, and threatened with prosecution if caught trespassing. In 1932 therefore, a mass demonstration was staged by over 600 ramblers who marched together over the Kinder Hill. The landowners confronted the demonstrators, and the police were forced to intervene. Although several of the ramblers were arrested and jailed, their plight had achieved its desired recognition and the restrictions were gradually relaxed. In 1951, when the National Park status was bestowed, the authorities made access agreements one of its main concerns.

The National Park is naturally divided into two distinct areas: the Dark Peak of the north and east, and the White Peak of the south. Both regions are on a limestone bedrock, but the Dark Peak moorlands are on coarse gritstone, which breaks through the surface of the peat to create rocky outcrops and edges. This gives the terrain a harsh, wild appearance. The green fields and rolling hills of the White Peak are in direct contrast. They are patterned with drystone walls, and divided by deep-cut dales.

Legend and folklore unsurprisingly abound in the Peak District. The Dark Peak in particular is the location for many sinister myths and mysteries. Perhaps the most famous of British legends to which the Peak District can lay a claim is the outlaw Robin Hood. The Peak Forest adjoined Sherwood Forest, and it is believed that Robin and his merry men indeed roamed the moors of the Peak District. The grave of Little John is to be found in the churchyard of Hathersage.

The population of the Peak District is 38,000, and millions of visitors are attracted to the park each year. Its hugely diverse landscape also provides a breadth of habitat to a wide range of rare plants and wildlife. In order to preserve these precious habitats and environments, approximately one third of the Peak District has been classed as a Site of Special Scientific Interest by English Nature, with two sections in particular designated as Environmentally Sensitive Areas.

Matlock Church and Riber Castle

Portsmouth Historic Dockyard

Portsmouth has been home to the British Navy for the greater part of the nation's maritime history, and is still one of the most important naval and defence bases in Europe. Portsmouth Historic Dockyard represents the past, present and future of naval Britain, and is the resting place of three of the world's greatest historic ships.

H.M.S. Victory

Considered to be the most famous warship in the world, H.M.S. Victory was the flagship of Admiral Sir John Jervis at the Battle of Cape St. Vincent in February 1797, and of Horatio Nelson at the Battle of Trafalgar in October 1805. It was in this battle, and on the decks of the Victory that Vice Admiral Lord Nelson was fatally shot.

The Victory was commissioned in 1765 and built at a cost of £63,176. She is the last remaining eighteenth century warship in existence. As the flagship of the Second Sea Lord, Commander in Chief Naval Home Command, she is also the longest serving Royal Navy ship in commission, and still has her own crew.

She serves today as a tribute to Nelson and to his victory at Trafalgar. In a bad condition, but still afloat, she was spared from demolition and converted to museum use in 1922.

Mary Rose

The Mary Rose was Henry VIII's favourite warship. The 700-tonne vessel was built in 1509, but survived only 36 years, sinking in the Solent in 1545. Her crew of 700 men perished.

Her wreck was discovered almost 300 years later in 1836, but not accurately located until 1967. In 1971, her hull was sighted below layers of the Solent's silt, and the world's largest excavation was recorded, with a team of over 600, comprising divers, archaeologists and scientists, working on the site.

On October 11, 1982, after 437 years on the sea bed, the Mary Rose was raised. The event was televised and broadcast to millions of viewers worldwide. What remained of the warship was taken back to Portsmouth Dockyard, and the artefacts recovered from the silt were used to piece together a picture of the Mary Rose and of the men who lived and died on her.

The restoration of the Mary Rose is a long and extremely controlled process. The remains of the hull and stern are sprayed continuously with cold fresh water, and in 1994, work began on the hull's permanent conservation.

H.M.S. Warrior

The most recent of the three historic ships at Portsmouth, the revolutionary Warrior was at the cutting edge of the naval technology of her time. Her main guns, engines and boilers operated from within an armoured iron hull. She could be powered by either steam or wind, and could outsail and defeat any enemy vessel on the sea. H.M.S. Warrior is a fine example of life on a navy ship in the Victorian era.

Although at the forefront of naval and combat technology when she was first introduced, the Warrior was soon overtaken by increasingly technical naval advances. When she had become obsolete, she finished her service as a floating oil jetty, before being completely restored and returned to Portsmouth in 1987.

The Mary Rose (right) defeats an Algerian Man-of-War

H.M.S. Warrior

Roman Baths

The hot springs and reputedly curative waters of Bath have been attracting people to the city for thousands of years. From the Iron Age settlers, to the Romans, and subsequently the high society of the eighteenth and nineteenth centuries, visitors have eagerly come to the city to take the waters. Today, Bath's fortunes still revolve around the baths as the tourism which they generate provides a generous source of revenue for the city.

According to legend, the city of Bath was founded by the Celtic King Bladud following a bath in the muddy swamp waters which supposedly cured him of leprosy. The Romans in the first century took over the native British sanctuary dedicated to the goddess Sulis, converting it into a sanctuary to Sulis-Minerva. The Romans too recognised the medicinal properties of the waters of Bath and consequently truly developed Bath into one of Roman Britain's most fashionable towns.

In contrast to all other towns occupied by the Romans, Bath was not developed as a garrison, but rather a sanctuary of rest and relaxation. Bathing was an extremely important event in the daily life of the Romans. In addition to their obvious cleansing functions, the baths also presented the Romans with an environment in which they could socialise, exercise, conduct business, trade or simply relax. The grander bathing establishments even incorporated libraries and lecture halls. The bathing area was accessible to Romans from all social spheres and was frequented by military generals of the Roman army and shopkeepers alike.

Bath is positioned between the Cotswold Hills to the north, and the Mendips to the south. 250,000 gallons of water, at a constant temperature of 46.5 degrees, flow from the springs daily. On the site of these hot springs the Romans constructed a complex of baths and a temple dedicated to the goddess Sulis-Minerva, after whom the town took its Roman name, Aquae Sulis, in 44AD. The proximity of the temple to the bath houses reflects the Roman belief that building temples close to places of importance would bestow fortune upon them. By the

The head of Sulis-Minerva

reign of Agricola in 78–84, the spa complex was extensive and extremely prosperous.

The temple of Sulis-Minerva would have been an incredible sight to behold. Pilgrims would approach the sacred spring, through its steam haze, in the centre of the temple, and therein throw their offerings to the goddess. By doing so, they believed that they were not only being touched by the healing powers of the waters, but that they were also able to communicate with the underworld. Almost 20,000 coins and artefacts have been recovered from this site.

In addition to the five hot baths which were contained within the complex at Bath, there were also a number of cold baths, swimming pools and sweat rooms. Centrally located in its own hall was the Great Bath, 26 m (85 ft) long and over 1.5 m (5 ft) deep, lined with 14 sheets of lead mined in the Mendip hills which lay to the south of the city. Its barrel vaulted roof prevented the formation of condensation and therefore protected the bathers beneath from the irritation of falling drops of water. It is undoubtedly the most spectacular feature of the complex.

Flooding was the eventual downfall of the Roman baths and temple. The rising level of the waters of the River Avon, into which the baths drained, eventually reached such a height that the river water began to flood back into the drains, clogging them up with mud and silt. With the Roman withdrawal from Britain in the fourth century, the baths were not restored, and fell into ruin.

It was not until the end of the seventeenth century that Bath began to recover its fashionable status, and the number of people travelling to the city to 'take the cure' increased. When Queen Anne visited the city in 1702, it instantly regained recognition and began to expand. By the eighteenth and nineteenth centuries, Bath had once again become a major spa and holiday centre and many of the fine Georgian buildings, which also characterise Bath, date from this period. Towards the end of the nineteenth century, sea bathing was proving to be a more popular trend, and the spa waters of Bath fell out of fashion.

Royal Albert Hall

The Royal Albert Hall of Arts and Sciences was completed and opened in 1871, exactly a decade after the death of its creator, Albert, the Prince Consort. His vision had been to build a central focus for a national incentive to promote the arts and sciences. This incentive included the founding of a collection of institutions all with this same goal and all to be located within a 50 acre area in South Kensington. This area had been transformed by the end of the 1800s, and now houses a number of London's most prestigious museums and colleges, as well as the Hall itself.

Although the Prince died before the commencement of the Hall, his ideas had been firmly established and the project was therefore taken over by his good friend Henry Cole, who had previously worked with the Prince on many other developments. He was aided by a Corporation which was set up in 1867, charged with the erection and maintenance of the Hall. Construction then began, and four years later, in the presence of the Prince's widow, Queen Victoria, the Hall was officially opened.

The original plan of creating the Hall to resemble a Coliseum was rejected due to the impractical implications. The idea was then modified so that the Hall still resembled a Roman amphitheatre but accommodated only 7,000 people. This seating capacity was later reduced to 5,500 for reasons of comfort and safety. At the time of its construction, the Hall's characteristic dome was the largest in the world. The red brick and terracotta outside walls of the Hall display the famous 243 m (800 ft) mosaic frieze. Architecturally, the Hall is of outstanding importance, and this is reflected in its status as a Grade I listed building.

The Royal Charter, which was set up in 1867 and under the terms of which the Corporation was appointed, still regulates the Hall. Although classed as a national institution, the Hall is completely self-governing, and has no recognised connections with, or funding from, either central or local government, despite the objectives behind the creation of the Hall being solely created in the public's interest.

Originally reliant on being hired out in order to meet the financial demands of maintenance and repairs, the Hall has, over the years, hosted a hugely varied and eclectic range of events which have forced it to maximise its potential. In the 1870s it was staging displays of innovative new developments, such as Morse Code and electric lighting, as well as fulfilling its original purpose of being a venue for the arts, most notably hosting the Wagner Festival conducted by Wagner himself.

'Last Night of the Proms' at the Royal Albert Hall

Throughout the twentieth century the Hall proved itself to be a venue for all occasions. The early 1900s saw the introduction of sport into the Hall, with the first wrestling contests and amateur boxing competitions. As well as being the venue for an orchestra of 500 performers, conducted by Edward Elgar, Henry Wood and Thomas Beecham, the Hall also staged a complete theatrical performance of Coleridge-Taylor's Hiawatha, the first all-British Wireless Festival, the Ford Motor Show, the first Proms session, television broadcasts (the first one being by Winston Churchill and Lord Montgomery), and was the venue for Suffragette rallies. As the century progressed pop concerts arrived at the Hall, Ronnie and Reggie Kray appeared in boxing bills, trade fairs were held, and Malcolm Sargent saw his last Last Night of the Proms.

The Hall underwent some refurbishment in 1971 as a result of a centenary appeal, and then further extended its repertoire to tennis tournaments, ice skating and even the first Sumo tournament to be held outside of Japan. The performing arts continue to feature prominently at the Royal Albert Hall, and famous names from opera and ballet never cease to draw in phenomenal crowds.

Royal Pavilion, Brighton

I t was the fashionable pastime of sea-bathing which first attracted the Prince of Wales to the village of Brighthelmstone, later Brighton, in 1783. Three years later he leased a small farmhouse close to the sea, which he commissioned the architect Henry Holland to enlarge in 1787. Holland transformed the house into a neo-classical villa with a domed central rotunda. It was named the Marine Pavilion of His Royal Highness.

In 1812, Prince George became Regent, and charged John Nash, his Surveyor-General, with the reconstruction of the building. Nash transformed the property into its current Indian style between 1815 and 1823. The external appearance of a mogul's palace was achieved by the addition of the domes, pinnacles and minarets. Internally, large amounts of money were lavished on the kitchen, entrance hall, long gallery and state apartments. This sumptuous interior was decorated in the Chinese style. Friendly critics called the Pavilion 'one of the most dazzling and exotic buildings in Europe'. Stern Victorians however, thought of it as both 'grotesque and oriental'. One of the most dramatic areas of the Pavilion is the Banqueting Room, the ceiling of which resembles a huge palm tree, and suspends a spectacular central chandelier held by a silvered dragon. It was in the rich opulence of this room that the lavish menus created in the Great Kitchen were served.

The Pavilion was subsequently used by both William IV and Queen Victoria. Victoria however, disliked the property, and felt that it lacked privacy. In 1845, the Pavilion was closed as a royal residence, and much of its furniture was dispersed. Within five years, the property had been bought by Brighton Corporation, and many of the furnishings, paintings and objets d'art have been gradually returned to it on permanent loan by generations of the Royal Family.

In 1975, the Royal Pavilion suffered unexpected damage when a fire bomb was thrown into the music room. A big effort was made to restore the Music Room to its former glory. The clergyman at Saint Peter's Church was so alarmed by this act of vandalism that he set up an all-night vigil to ensure that Brighton's monument to Regency Britain did not come under further attack.

A full programme of restoration of the Royal Pavilion began in 1982 and extensive external structural and interior restoration was carried out on the building. Nash's roof, which had been poorly designed and was not at all weatherproof, underwent considerable renovation. Magnificent decorations and fantastic furnishings were recreated and the Pavilion is now filled with mythical creatures, astonishing colours and superb craftsmanship.

Outside, the Gardens are restored to the original Regency planting scheme and design.

In October 1987, not long after the structural restoration was completed, The Great Storm, which tore down trees and buildings across the south east of England, knocked one of the large domes through the roof into the newly restored music room, damaging it once more. The Music Room has now been lovingly restored and the present Royal Family has donated generously to the furniture and ornaments now on display.

Salisbury Cathedral

Salisbury Cathedral is unique in its design as, unlike the majority of Britain's medieval cathedrals, it was planned as a single unit and not constructed in stages over many centuries. The construction of the cathedral began in 1220 and was completed in 1266, the only exception being the spire which was added in 1334. Much of the cathedral's glory is in its magnificent 123 m (404 ft) high spire, the tallest in England. The Cathedral itself was built entirely in the Early English Gothic style and is one of the most beautiful cathedrals in Britain.

Originally, the cathedral for the region was in the town of Old Sarum, approximately 302 km (2 miles) north of Salisbury. This cathedral was completed in 1092, but was immediately badly damaged by a lightning bolt. Although the cathedral was eventually rebuilt in 1130, the bishops felt that its location was unsatisfactory. They claimed that the cathedral's position on top of a hill posed problems for the supply of water to the building, that the weather ailed the monks and that the congregation's singing could not be heard for the strong winds to which the cathedral was completely exposed. A petition was sent to the Pope in 1217 requesting that the cathedral be moved to a more suitable location, and thus in 1220 the construction of Salisbury Cathedral, to be built on the plains and in the proximity of three rivers, began.

Trinity Chapel, at the eastern end of the cathedral, was the first structure to be completed, and was finished in 1225. In the following year, the shrine of St. Osmund was installed in the chapel. Osmund had been responsible for the completion of the original cathedral at Old Sarum at the end of the eleventh century, but was not canonised until 1457. In 1258, the main part of the church was completed, and by 1266, the entire building was finished and the cloisters were added. The cloisters now lead to the Chapter House, built between 1263 and 1284, in which is contained one of the four original versions of the Magna Carta, the agreed recognition of rights which was drawn up between the barons and King John in 1215 and which established that everyone, including the lawmakers and the king himself, was to be answerable to the law.

The beautiful spire was added at the end of the thirteenth century. As this was an unplanned addition, the four central piers of the cathedral were not strong enough to hold the extra 6,400 tonnes which the spire brought. These stone piers are each 2 m^2 (21.5 ft²), but the colossal weight of the spire has forced the huge columns to bend. The curve is most visible on the eastern piers. Supportive buttresses have been added to the interior and exterior of the building, and the maintenance and careful monitoring of the spire has been conducted thoroughly for centuries and continues to the present day. The spire itself however, is believed not to have moved at all. A survey conducted by Sir Christopher Wren in 1668 revealed that the spire was actually leaning sideways by 75 centimetres. In 1737, the measurement was taken again, and the spire proved to be in exactly the same position as it had been when Wren had first calculated this angle. Subsequent surveys in the twentieth century showed that the spire has still not moved any further.

Salisbury is also renowned for its cathedral close. In 1333, the close was walled in using materials taken from the original cathedral at Old Sarum, and physically separated from the town. Thus it remains and is locked every evening, only to be opened by the key-holding residents, one of whom is the former prime minister, Edward Heath.

Second Severn Crossing

There has, since the remotest time, been a river crossing from England into Wales. Remains of boats in the Welsh mud flats show that there were ferries long before the Romans arrived. The ferries crossed at the narrowest point of the Severn Estuary, where the modern bridges are. The Romans forded the Sabrine, further upstream, where many fine bridges are recorded to have been constructed later in the thirteenth and fourteenth centuries, but these have all succumbed to the ravages of floods, wars and time itself.

Today there are two main bridges which carry traffic across the river Severn. The Severn Suspension Bridge, which originally carried the M4 and was constructed as an alternative to the ferry service, was built in 1966, and its new neighbour, the Second Severn Crossing, which was completed in 1996. It is now across the latter that the M4 makes its way westwards from England into Wales.

By the 1980s, the volume of traffic on the original Severn Bridge was causing severe congestion, and when accidents or dangerous weather conditions forced the bridge to close, traffic had to be diverted via Gloucester.

The Second Severn Crossing was designed fundamentally to provide road traffic with an alternative route and thereby ease congestion. A study commissioned by the government in 1984 concluded that an increase in the number of traffic lanes was necessary, and that by reducing the congestion on the roads into Wales, the increasing prosperity of South Wales would be safeguarded and would continue into the twenty-first century. Two years later therefore, the agreement was made between the Secretaries of State for Transport and for Wales that a second bridge would be constructed. The new bridge would be built close to the line of the Railway Tunnel and would carry the M4 across the Severn Estuary from both banks. Following extensive planning and discussions in both England and Wales, Royal Assent was finally granted to the Severn Bridges Act in 1992.

The site chosen for the bridge certainly presented a number of challenges for the team charged with its construction. The bridge's location in such an exposed area necessitated a design which would make it strong enough to withstand the heavy sea winds which blow up the estuary from the sea. The bridge however, had to be made strong in a way which would not make it any less aesthetically pleasing. An additional problem was the 14.5 m (47.5 ft) tidal range of the estuary. To prevent any difficulties which this may have presented, the construction team pre-cast and pre-stressed the concrete on shore and transported it by specialist equipment on to the estuary.

The completed bridge was cable-stayed with a main span of 465 m (1,525 ft) and supported by two concrete piers. The entire length of the bridge is 5.2 km (3 miles). 240 stay cables were used on either side, and 2,300 match-cast units formed the two viaducts. The Second Severn Crossing won the British Construction Industry Civil Engineering Award and Supreme Award 1996, and is the first structure of its size designed to include full wind protection for the traffic.

Shakespeare's Birthplace

William Shakespeare is arguably the greatest playwright and poet of all time. Simply for being his birthplace, the small market town of Stratford-upon-Avon quickly became the most famous and most visited literary landmark of Britain. Of particular interest to tourists and literati is the timber-framed house on Henley Street where the great bard is believed to have been born.

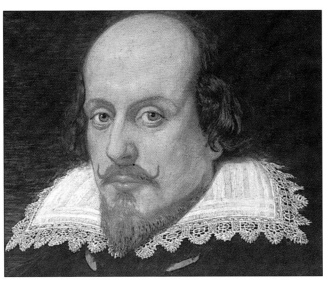
William Shakespeare 1564–1616

Shakespeare's family originally lived in the nearby village of Snitterfield where his grandfather, Richard, rented land from Robert Arden. By 1552, William's father, John, had moved from Snitterfield to Stratford where he began a profitable career as a wool merchant and in 1557 he married Mary Arden, the daughter of his father's landlord. His continued success at work enabled him to buy the house on Henley Street as a family home.

Of the eight children born to John and Mary Shakespeare, William was the third. Although neither the exact date nor the exact location of William's birth can be confirmed, his birth was registered as 'April 1564'. He was baptised on April 26, an event which normally occurred within a week of the birth. As it was on this same day in 1616 that he died, and as it also happened to be St. George's Day, April 23 is traditionally observed as his birthday. The house on Henley Street is considered to be his birthplace as this was the property in which his parents were residing at the time.

Shakespeare certainly spent his formative years in the house, and as a result of his father's continued business success he was sent to the local grammar school to receive his education. It is likely to have been at this school that both his literary interests and talent were cultivated.

The house which stands on Henley Street today has undergone heavy restoration and has emerged with subtle differences from the one in which Shakespeare lived. The striking black and white half timbered façade was bricked over in the eighteenth century and re-exposed in the nineteenth, and the houses which stood either side of the building were destroyed in order to avoid the risk of spreading fire to the historically

important birthplace. The inside of the house is more authentic, although the oak beams and stone have been restored and the house has been re-furnished with contemporary Elizabethan furniture. It has been carefully designed to closely resemble the house as Shakespeare would have known it.

The house remained in the Shakespeare family until 1847, when it passed to the Shakespeare Birthday Committee, who conducted the restoration and transformed it into a national monument, a decision fully supported by the public. The house subsequently became a site of pilgrimage for tourists and has remained so for more than two centuries since. The glass of a window in what is believed to have been Shakespeare's birth room bears the engraved signatures of some of the house's earliest nineteenth century visitors. In 1891, Shakespeare's Birthplace Trust was established and charged with the administration of the house. Later added to their charge were Anne Hathaway's Cottage and Mary Arden's House.

William Shakespeare statue in Stratford-upon-Avon

Silverstone

Formerly a World War II hilltop airfield, Silverstone will always be remembered in the history of Formula One racing as the location for the first ever round of the official world championship in 1950. Its active history as a racing circuit predates this by two years when, in 1948, it began its racing life as the host for the first British Grand Prix. It has been considered to be the home of the race ever since. Silverstone is one of the fastest circuits in Europe and has a lap record of over 225 km.p.h. (140 miles p.h.).

The 1948 circuit was created by a group of racing enthusiasts from the Royal Automobile Club who had selected the airfield track at Silverstone as the location for the first post-war Grand Prix. The circuit was marked out by the positioning of straw bales, and included both the runways and perimeter roads of the airfield.

This circuit was redesigned in 1949, and a course was set out which used only the perimeter roads in the lap. This course has changed a number of times, but is similar to the circuit in use today. This course was selected by Formula One, then called the World Championship for Drivers, and their first race was held there in 1950. The 1950 race was won by Giuseppe Farina, driving an Alfa Romeo. Victory then passed to Ferrari for the following four consecutive years.

From the mid 1950s, Silverstone shared its prestigious status as the home of the British Grand Prix with the newly built Aintree circuit. Aintree however, was no longer used after 1962, but Brands Hatch took its place, hosting its first race in 1964. Until 1986, when Brands Hatch staged its last race, the British Grand Prix alternated between there and Silverstone exclusively.

The first alterations to be made to the Silverstone course occurred in 1975, when in an attempt to reduce the speed of the cars, a chicane was added at Woodcote. This chicane was replaced twelve years later by a new complex which introduced Bridge Corner and Luffield to the lap, succeeded in slowing the cars down, and added 0.4 km (0.25 miles) to the total distance of each lap.

Tragedy struck Formula One in 1994, when the Brazilian driver Ayrton Senna was killed in a crash at the San Marino circuit in Italy. Although an inquiry into the accident concluded that it had been caused by faulty engineering, causing the steering column to snap, the repercussions of Senna's death were massive and safety was revised and improved at Grand Prix circuits worldwide.

The amendments made to the Silverstone track included slowing measures to the Woodcote, Becketts, Stowe and Copse corners. Additional improvements were made to the pits and paddock areas and a new medical centre with equipment valued at £500,000 was installed.

The manpower necessary to stage the British Grand Prix weekend is vast. Over 1,500 volunteer officials and marshals are on duty over the entire weekend. One of the non-sporting legends of Silverstone, and of Formula One racing, is the infectiously enthusiastic Murray Walker, race commentator and man responsible for introducing thousands of people to the sport. As famous for his propensity for making colossal errors as for his commentary itself, Walker retired from Formula One in 2001, having commentated on every race held at Silverstone since 1948. As he once said of a race held in Montreal, it's 'a sad ending, albeit a happy one'.

In 2001, the British Racing Drivers' Club, which had taken over the running of the circuit in 1951, leased Silverstone to Octagon Motorsports, thereby securing the future of the Formula One British Grand Prix at Silverstone until 2015.

South Downs

To traverse the South Downs is to cross one of the most beautifully diverse and historically significant landscapes of Great Britain. The area forms a rich tapestry of undulating ridges, woodlands, valleys, chalk cliffs, rivers, hamlets and villages. The landscape is permeated by centuries of history, and has borne witness to the lives, cultures and developments of Great Britain's earliest civilisations, the few remains of which have been investigated by historians and archaeologists. Thousands of years of human activity has undoubtedly moulded the land over these centuries, yet the wild and natural beauty of the countryside still prevails.

The first tracks of the South Downs were probably made by the first farmers, who lived in dispersed farmsteads but came together for occasional meetings in great enclosures. The biggest of these were The Trundle at Goodwood and Whitehawk at Brighton. Concentrations of long barrows, built around 3500 BC, also suggest that there were two major tribal groups, one in West Sussex and one in East Sussex. Between the two, north of Worthing, neolithic communities mined first for their axes and knives. Enclosures were built in the Iron Age, possibly for ceremonial use, but also, as the threat from Rome increased, as fortified refuges. Mount Caburn above Lewes is a fine example.

When the Romans invaded at the beginning of the first century, they built military roads which crossed the South Downs from the coast to London. These roads were well built and engineered, and consequently remain as the basis of roads, footpaths and bridleways in use twenty centuries later.

When the Romans departed Britain, the Saxons claimed the land and set up their own farms and villages, often around springs at the foot of the escarpment to ensure a reliable water supply. The Saxon communities remained, even after the final invasion of Britain by William Duke of Normandy in 1066.

From the eleventh century, the highways across the Downs fell into disuse, and the area became wild and barren. By the seventeenth and eighteenth centuries, sheep rearing had become the prime industry. With the outbreak of the Second World War however, the lush, green, grazed pastures of the South Downs were used as training areas for the tanks, guns and armoured vehicles of the British forces. Large areas were also extensively ploughed for mass food production. The wild and natural beauty was destroyed and, even after the conclusion of the war, never fully restored to its former glory. Instead, tractors and combine harvesters appeared and much of the land became arable fields. Farmers today, however, are being encouraged to return to Downland pasture and sheep grazing.

A popular rambling route, the South Downs Way is a National Trail which covers 161 km (100 miles) of ancient routes and paths along the ridges and chalk cliffs of the Downs. The track begins in Eastbourne in East Sussex and terminates at Winchester in Hampshire and is characterised by the rolling chalk cliffs, deep valleys and extensive views over the countryside and out to sea. Recognised as an area of exceptional beauty, and of rare habitats, species and wildlife, the South Downs are now carefully monitored and protected by environmental bodies.

St. Andrews Golf Course

Although the beautiful seaside town of St. Andrews was once the ecclesiastical capital of Scotland, its castle and cathedral both now lie in ruins and the town is internationally renowned as the home of golf. It is the location of the world's most famous golf course, the Old Course, and is the headquarters of the game's governing body, the Royal and Ancient Golf Club.

The history of golf at St. Andrews dates back over six hundred years to the fifteenth century. So popular was this sport at that time that in 1457 a ban was placed on it by James II who objected to the precedence that it was beginning to take over his troops' archery practice. This ban continued to be enforced by successive monarchs until the reign of James IV who was attracted by the sport and became a keen golfer himself.

The Old Course dates back to the sixteenth century, and contrary to popular belief, is a public course and is open to anybody who wishes to play on it. Its popularity often hinders a booking, but the course itself, unlike its neighbour, the all-male Royal and Ancient Golf Course, is not exclusive.

The Royal and Ancient Club House at St. Andrews

It was on the Old Course that the standard round of 18 holes was created. Originally, the course had 22 holes, 11 in total, but golfers played the same holes on the way out as the way back. It was generally agreed by the golfers that the first, and last, four holes were too short, and that they should be lengthened by playing just two of the four holes. Consequently, the game changed from 22 holes to 18.

The 'double green' was also first introduced on the Old Course. With the increase in the numbers of golfers on the course, due to the game's rising popularity, problems were arising with those going out wanting to play the same hole as those

Tiger Woods plays the 18th hole at St. Andrews

coming in. To resolve the disputes and arguments which this was causing, an additional hole was cut on each green, with the outward holes marked by white flags, and the inward holes marked by red flags.

With the rapid growth in popularity of golf, the Royal and Ancient was established in 1754, making it one of the world's oldest clubs. It was originally named the Society of St Andrews Golfers, but changed its name in 1834 following the royal status it acquired when William IV was appointed as its first patron. Its imposing clubhouse was built a century later.

The Royal and Ancient was held in high esteem by other clubs at the end of the nineteenth century, and was consequently regarded as the ultimate authority on the rules of the game. This commonly recognised status became official in 1897 when the demand became strong for a standardised version of the rules. With the leading clubs looking to the Royal and Ancient for guidance, they established the first Rules of Golf Committee. Since the bestowal of this prestigious duty upon the R&A, it has been globally recognised as golf's official governing body for all countries except the U.S.A.

The British Open Championship has been held at St. Andrews since 1873, and it also hosts many of the important amateur contests including the Walker Cup and the Scottish Amateur Championships.

St. James's Palace

The royal residence of St. James's Palace is a building which is steeped in monarchic history. It was the residence of the kings and queens of England for three centuries, the place to which Queen Anne brought the court in 1702, the last confine of Charles I prior to his execution in 1649, the wedding location for Queen Victoria in 1840, and the palace in which Princess Beatrice was christened in 1988.

The site on which St. James's Palace was constructed was originally the site of the Hospital of St. James. The hospital was established in the twelfth century and provided care and refuge for those suffering from leprosy. The building came into the possession of Henry VIII in 1532 and due to its proximity to his official palace in Whitehall, Henry constructed in its

The Clarence House entrance to St. James's Palace

place a recreational royal palace and garden.

Little remains of the palace which Henry built, with the exception of the great turreted Tudor gatehouse, which still bears Henry's royal cipher, and the Chapel Royal. The court was brought to St. James's Palace by Queen Anne in 1702 following the devastating fire at the Palace of Whitehall. It then remained the palace of the sovereign until Queen Victoria's reign during which she moved to Buckingham Palace. It is still to the Court of St. James that foreign ambassadors and high commissioners are accredited.

The function of the Chapel Royal, created by Henry VIII, was for the priests and singers within it to serve the spiritual needs of the sovereign. It is now regarded as the birthplace of English church music and has an impressive register of noted organists and composers, amongst them Henry Purcell and George Frederick Handel. Handel was appointed by George II and composed the anthem *Zadok the Priest* for the sovereign's coronation, a piece which has been played at every coronation since.

Also on the palace grounds is Clarence House, commissioned by the Duke of Clarence, later King William IV, and built by John Nash in the nineteenth century. Clarence House was the London home of the late Queen Mother, and the place from which Diana left for St. Paul's Cathedral on her wedding day.

St. James's Palace has been the location for many nationally and historically important events. It was in the palace that Queen Mary signed the treaty which surrendered Calais, and from here that Queen Elizabeth I left to address famously the troops at Tilbury Camp during the troubles of the Spanish Armada. Charles II and James II were born at the palace, and George III and IV were married there. The coffin of Princess Diana lay at St. James's Palace, from whence it was taken to her funeral in Westminster Abbey.

Today, St. James's is a working palace, and also contains the residences of the Prince of Wales, and Princess Alexandra and her husband Sir Angus Ogilvy. The Royal Family use the state apartments for State and diplomatic events and these are also the headquarters of many charities, patronised by members of the Royal Family, and royal associations. For this reason, St. James's Palace is not accessible to the public.

Changing of the Guard at St. James's Palace

St. Michael's Mount

Considered to be the 'Jewel in Cornwall's Crown', St. Michael's Mount is an island just a few hundred yards out to sea from the shore of Marazion. It rises majestically from the water and reaches a height, measured from sea level to the top of the castle tower, of 70 m (230 ft).

St. Michael's Mount has very close links with its French counterpart, Mont St. Michel, in Normandy. It is believed that, having spent much of his time in France as a young boy, Edward the Confessor had been greatly influenced by the Norman monks. When he was consequently struck by the similarity of the two mounts he founded a chapel on St. Michael's Mount in 1044 and granted the land to the Benedictine monks of Mont St. Michel.

Mont St. Michel in Normandy, France

This is contested by some, who believe that the monks may have forged this charter in order to cement their claim on the land. A more popular explanation is that St. Michael's Mount was granted to the monks by Robert, Count of Mortain, after he had been awarded the title of 'Earl of Cornwall' by William the Conqueror after 1066. The Abbot of Mont St. Michel, Bernard of Le Bec, built the Benedictine Priory in 1135.

The Priory, in a perfect location for a fortress, subsequently became a fortified castle and was intermittently used in a military role. The Mount was first seized by King Richard's brother John and his supporters while the King was away on a Crusade in the twelfth century. With his declaration of war on France in the early fifteenth century, Henry V seized St. Michael's Mount as an alien priory and it became the property of the crown. The buildings were again used as fortresses during the Wars of the Roses, the Cornish Rebellion and the English Civil War. The purchase of the Mount by its last military governor, Sir John St. Aubin, in 1660 marked the beginning of a peaceful existence which it has enjoyed throughout the four centuries since.

Until the eighteenth century the house on the Mount was used only as a summer residence by the St. Aubin family. In the 1700s however, they began the conversion of this house into a more permanent residence. A new wing was added and Victorian apartments were built.

St. Michael's Mount remained the property of the St. Aubyn family until the third lord St. Levan gave the house and land to the National Trust in 1964. In addition to the church, house and exotic garden, there is now a harbour, restaurant and a collection of shops on St. Michael's Mount. At low tide it is possible to reach the Mount on foot across the causeway from Marazion. At high tide it can only be reached by ferry.

This romantic island location and the fairy-tale castle have given rise to a number of legends which now surround the Mount. The most popular of these is the story of the giant Cormoran, who waded ashore during the night to steal the grazing sheep and cows from the fields of Marzion. One day, while Cormoran slept, Jack, a local boy rowed out to the island and dug a huge pit into one of the slopes of the Mount. He then sounded a horn to wake the giant up. Cormoran came thundering down the slope and, failing to see the deep pit, fell straight into it. Jack was then heralded as a heroic giant killer, and the spot where he had dug the pit is now the well which is passed on the way up to the castle from the harbour.

St. Paul's Cathedral

Sir Christopher Wren's magnificent domed masterpiece, St. Paul's Cathedral, dominates the London skyline and from it panoramic views extend across the capital. One of London's most famous and recognisable landmarks, the impressive roof stood out as a beacon of hope in the midst of a war ravaged London. Believed by the Prince of Wales to have more impressive acoustics than those of Westminster Abbey, the cathedral featured on every newspaper across the world when the ill-fated marriage of Charles and Lady Diana took place there in 1981.

The history of the cathedral is an eventful one, and its origins date as far back as the turn of the seventh century, when a small wooden church was built on the site by Mellitus, Bishop of the East Saxons. When Mellitus's church was destroyed by fire, it was rebuilt in 675–85 by St. Erkenwald, then bishop of London. This new stone church stood for almost three centuries until the Vikings attacked and demolished the building.

A Norman church, named Old St. Paul's, was begun in the late eleventh century and took over 150 years to complete. Over the following centuries, amendments were made, including the installation of a new Gothic choir in 1313, and the addition of the tallest spire in Europe in the following year.

During the following three centuries, Old St. Paul's suffered much misfortune. A rampaging Protestant rabble vandalised the building and its contents in the mid-sixteenth century, the towering spire was struck by lightning, and general deterioration occurred when the building became a trade floor where merchants came to sell their wares. During the civil war, parliamentary troops took over the site and used the nave as their barracks.

When the monarchy was restored in 1660, Old St. Paul's faced a much brighter future. The architect Christopher Wren was appointed by Charles II to carry out the necessary repairs to the cathedral. This he began, but tragedy struck when he was only a short way into this task. When the Great Fire of London spread throughout the city, destroying over 13,000 buildings, Old St. Paul's was amongst those which were burnt off the London map. In its place were scorched timbers and debris.

From tragedy however, was born incredible opportunity. As the smoke was clearing across London, Wren was already remodelling the streets of the city in revolutionary plans. The King thoroughly approved of his designs for wide avenues and open plazas, but the people of London had already commenced the task of rebuilding their homes and businesses in the same locations as they had previously stood. This idea therefore had to be abandoned and Wren was instead charged with the redesign of the churches of the city, amongst them Old St. Paul's.

He submitted several plans and his third was chosen in 1675. His favourite design was an imposing, equal-armed Greek cross, but this was rejected as too revolutionary. Wren is said to have wept. His final proposal was that of a traditional English church with a long nave and spire. Perhaps to grant Wren a degree of freedom to introduce a more modern touch to this traditional design, the royal approval was given by Charles who specified that Wren was allowed to make variations to the design, 'rather ornamental than essential'. Wren then proceeded to change almost every feature of his original proposal.

The cathedral was constructed in Portland stone and was completed in an incredible 33 years. It is an outstanding example of the creativity and originality of its architect. Sir Christopher Wren's tomb is amongst the memorials, including those to Lord Nelson and Lawrence of Arabia, within St. Paul's Cathedral and the Latin inscription chosen by his son simply reads, LECTOR, SI MONUMENTUM REQUIRIS, CIRCUMSPICE, which translates as, *Reader, if you seek his monument, look around you.*

Stonehenge

The megalithic ruin known as Stonehenge stands on the open downland of Salisbury Plain 3 km (2 miles) west of the town of Amesbury, Wiltshire, in Southern England. It is not a single structure but consists of a series of earth, timber and stone structures that were revised and re-modelled over a period of more than 6,000 years.

The earliest phase was the erection of a line of totem poles across the site of the Stonehenge car park. These posts were raised over several centuries between 8100 BC and 7100 BC.

The earliest part of the main site is the circular bank and ditch about 100 m (328 ft) in diameter. Just inside the earth bank, with its two entrances, is a circle of 56 Aubrey Holes which originally held wooden posts. This phase was built 3000–2900 BC, and also included a complicated timber setting in the middle which may have been a roundhouse.

Posts were set up and taken down at the north east entrance, apparently connected with observations of the moonrise. The entrance was marked with a pair of portal stones, of which only one, the Heel Stone, survives. These were to mark the midsummer sunrise.

From 2500 BC, the monument underwent a complicated sequence of settings of large stones. The first stone setting comprised a series of 80 Bluestones, brought from Preseli in Wales, and placed in what are known as the Q and R Holes. These were dismantled shortly afterwards and a circle of Sarsens and a horseshoe-shaped arrangement of Trilithons erected in 2450 BC.

The Sarsen Circle, about 33 m (108 ft) in diameter, comprised 30 neatly trimmed upright sandstone blocks of which only seventeen are now standing. The stones, raised in 2400 BC, are evenly spaced approximately 1–1.4 m (3.2–4.6 ft) apart, and stand on average 4 m (13 ft) above the ground. They are about 2 m (6.5 ft) wide and 1 m (3 ft) thick and taper towards the top. They originally supported sarsen lintels forming a continuous circle around the top. Each lintel block has been shaped to the curve of the circle. The average length of the rectangular lintels is 3.2 m (10 ft 6 in). The Bluestones were reincorporated within the Sarsen monument in 2150 BC.

There are many outlying monuments, such as barrow clusters, processional ways and the remains of roundhouses (such as Woodhenge). The hope is that by closing or diverting the roads near Stonehenge, the ancient prehistoric landscape may be seen once again as a powerful unity.

Thames Barrier

The Thames Barrier has been described as the eighth wonder of the world – it is certainly a very impressive work of engineering.

High water level at London Bridge has risen about 0.76 m (2.5 ft) per century, due to the melting of the polar ice caps and the activities of Man. However, the main possible cause of flooding in the London area is surge tides. These originate in the North Atlantic, and generally pass to the north of the British Isles. Occasionally, however, northerly winds will force them into the North Sea, sending millions of tonnes of extra water up the Thames. 1,250,000 people were at risk, spread over 116.5 km² (45 miles²).

In 1953 a particularly disastrous flood occurred. Over 300 people drowned and about 160,000 acres on Canvey Island, near the mouth of the Thames, were covered in sea water. The government appointed a committee to look at the flood problem. One of the recommendations was that a barrier be erected across the Thames. The main problem was that the volume of shipping using London Docks was at its peak, and that ships were getting bigger. This meant that an opening in the barrier of around 426 m (1,400 ft) would be required. A number of schemes were put forward, but failed to come to fruition.

Then the whole system of sea transportation began to change. Cargo began to be shipped in containers on purpose-built ships, and a new container port was opened downstream at Tilbury. The old London Docks became redundant. It was decided that openings only 60 m (200 ft) wide, the same as Tower Bridge, would be sufficient, and the site of the barrier could be further upstream than originally envisaged.

Finally, work on building the barrier started in 1974. It was designed for the Greater London Council by Rendel, Palmer and Tritton, and was officially opened by H.M. Queen Elizabeth II on May 8, 1984. The 523 m (1,716 ft) width of the river is divided by nine reinforced concrete piers, to form six openings for shipping and four other openings. The piers are founded on solid chalk, over 15 m (50 ft) below the level of the river. The four largest steel gates are 60 m (200 ft) wide and weigh 1,500 tonnes each. 4,000 men and women were engaged in the building work, which cost nearly £500,000,000. In addition, 18.5 km (11.5 miles) of the river, to the east of the barrier, were protected by new walls, to a new defence level of 7 m (23 ft). New walkways and amenity areas were created. This further work cost around £100,000,000. Similar work was carried out by other Water Authorities, improving the defences to the mouth of the estuary.

However, this mighty Thames Barrier is only a stop-gap measure. Britain continues to tilt towards the south-east at a rate of 0.3 m (1 ft) every 100 years and the polar ice caps continue to melt. The sea, therefore, continues to rise: presently at about the rate of 0.6 m (2ft) every century. We gather to admire the spectacle of these 19 m (65 ft) high, 3,000-tonne gates holding back the vast wall of water on the east side while, on the west, canoeists frolic in the extemporised rapids of that fraction that is allowed underneath the gates.

In 1907 and in 1928 a barrage at Gravesend was proposed, but it was as a result of the 1953 floods during which over 300 people were drowned and 65,000 hectares (160,000 acres) of farmland were flooded with salt water, that the Government appointed a committee under the chairmanship of Lord Waverley. Several schemes were proposed and rejected and it was only after the formation of the Greater London Council (GLC) in 1965 that government consent was given to build a barrier. The design was chosen from 41 proposals because it minimises interference with the natural flow of the river, does not pose a headroom restriction for shipping, is attractive and practical. Charles Draper was the engineer whose idea for radial gates which are normally parked flat below the bed of the river, evolved from the working principle of a domestic gas-tap.

500,000 tonnes of concrete were used in the coffer dams inside which the piers were built, and also in the sills on which the gates rest on the river bed when not in service. When raised, each of the four main gates is as high as a five-storey building and as wide as the opening of Tower Bridge and, with the two gate arms, weighs 3,700 tonnes. The hydraulic power packs are electrically driven, using three alternative supplies, routed via each of the river banks from three on-site power generators.

Tower Bridge

At the end of the nineteenth century, the rapidly expanding city of London was suffering seriously from traffic congestion. In August 1882, a census conducted at London Bridge, the only easterly crossing over the Thames, revealed that over a two day period, the bridge was crossed by more than 22,000 vehicles and 100,000 pedestrians. Journeys were being delayed by hours, and the need for a new bridge was becoming a matter of extreme urgency.

In addition to the increase in road traffic however, there was an increase in the volume of river traffic using the Thames. London was a thriving port and no bridge could be allowed to prevent the passage of the ships and boats that used the river to reach London's docks.

To find a solution to this apparently unsolvable dilemma, the 'Special Bridge or Subway Committee' was formed in 1876. They launched a competition for the public to propose the ideal design for the new crossing.

Of approximately 50 suggested designs, the one eventually chosen was submitted by the engineer John Wolfe Barry and the city architect, Sir Horace Jones. Jones unfortunately died in the same year that the pair were commissioned to construct the bridge.

The design was that of a bascule bridge, the largest and most sophisticated of its time, and it was to be located over the river by the Tower of London. The bridge was to be hydraulically operated, using steam to power the massive pumping engines. The energy could then be stored so that it was ready to lift the bridge as soon as the ships approached. The bridge was also constructed to adhere to strict specifications regarding the amount of clearance necessary for the passing ships. The bridge was designed to allow a clear width of 60 m (200 ft) and a clear height of 41 m (135 ft) when raised. The maximum angle to which the bridge could be raised was 86 degrees.

The bridge was built in the Gothic style. The two cornish stone towers, from which the bridge takes its name, serve no purpose other than that of decoration and were designed to complement the Tower of London. The walkway above the bridge was installed for use by pedestrians when the bridge itself needed to be raised. However, this feature soon became redundant as pedestrians preferred to wait the five minutes which it took for the bridge to rise and lower.

The first stone of Tower Bridge was laid by the Prince of Wales, who then officially opened the structure when it had been completed in 1894. It took a total of eight years and over 400 construction workers to complete Tower Bridge. 11,000 tonnes of steel were used for the framework of the towers and walkways, and two massive piers were deposited on to the river bed to support the structure. Cornish granite and Portland stone were then applied to the steel both to protect it, and to provide the desired aesthetic appearance.

When Tower Bridge first opened over a century ago, it was being raised approximately 50 times a day to allow ships to pass underneath. It now operates much less frequently. Since 1976, the bascules have been powered by oil and electricity in place of the steam power originally used.

Tower Bridge is one of London's most famous landmarks, and is a very popular tourist attraction. One group of American purchasers were so taken by Tower Bridge that when they heard that is was for sale they made an offer on it which was accepted. Unfortunately, they had confused Tower Bridge with London Bridge and they were less than satisfied when the structure was reassembled and not the spectacular two-towered construction they believed they had bought. London Bridge now connects the mainland and island of Lake Havasu City in Arizona.

The Bridge rises and lowers to allow ships to pass underneath

Tower of London

The Tower of London has played a myriad of roles in the millennium since its construction. It has served as protector, jailer, executioner and host. It has been both the residence of monarchs and, for some, their final prison. It is enshrouded in political intrigue yet entrusted with priceless treasures. The lions and bears which were once confined in the grounds of the Tower have now left, but the flightless ravens remain. Their wings are clipped so that they may never fulfil the prophecy which states that the day they fly from the Tower, London will fall to its enemies.

Following the Norman invasion of England in 1066, William the Conqueror began the construction of a number of forts in important locations across the country. One of these was built on the north bank of the River Thames on the south-eastern edge of London. A huge stone stronghold, its purpose was to symbolise his power, imprison his foes and defend his land.

When the Tower of London was completed at the end of the eleventh century, it rose to a height of almost 30 m (100 ft), and in places, its walls were 4.5m (15ft) thick. In later years a wide ditch and surrounding wall were installed which both protected the Tower and ensured that no prisoners could escape its confines.

Henry III moved into the Tower in the mid-thirteenth century and made several modifications to the building and its grounds. He expanded the area of the Tower to include a church and a great hall and transformed the central keep, which he had whitewashed, into a palace in which he could entertain important guests.

Richard II encountered turmoil during his time at the Tower of London. He and his court were forced to seek refuge within the stronghold when the Tower was stormed by angry overtaxed farm labourers. Although unable to find the king,

The Yeomen of the Guard, commonly known as 'Beefeaters'

the peasants dragged the Archbishop of Canterbury and the Royal Treasurer to Tower Hill where they executed them. Richard himself was thrown into one of the dungeons of the Tower at the end of his reign when he was forced to abdicate to Henry IV.

One of the most fiercely debated subjects in British history is the fate of the two princes, one of whom, Edward V, was the uncrowned King of England. It is widely believed that their uncle, Richard III, ordered their murder in the Garden Tower, now renamed the Bloody Tower.

When Henry VII defeated Richard III at the

The Bloody Tower, the alleged scene of Richard's murder of the two princes

Battle of Bosworth Field in 1485, he moved into the Tower of London. Fearing for his safety, the king formed a personal bodyguard of protectors. These were the Yeoman of the Guard, who still remain a feature of the Tower, dressed in their characteristic Tudor style, and who serve to protect the Tower of London and its residents.

When Henry VII died, the Tower was never again to serve as a residence for a British monarch. It did however, continue its role as the final place of incarceration prior to execution for many of the monarch's prisoners, and occasionally royalty themselves. Amongst those who spent their final night in the Tower were Sir Thomas More, Catherine Howard, Lady Jane Grey and Walter Raleigh. Some were beheaded within the precincts of the Tower, and some on the neighbouring Tower Hill. Anne Boleyn was executed at the Tower exactly three years after her marriage to Henry VIII had taken place at the same location.

In 1603, James I ordered that the Crown Jewels be displayed in the Tower Jewel House. They remain in the Tower to the present day, but are now on show to visitors in the Waterloo Barracks.

Trafalgar Square

Trafalgar Square is at the very heart of the city of London, and is the place from which 'all distances are measured'. It is the site of great rallies and marches, and the annual destination for thousands of New Year's revellers. Nelson famously presides over the square from atop a huge 56 m (185 ft) granite column, at the corners of the base of which sit four giant bronze lions. Tourists, Londoners and the famous pigeons flock to the square in equal numbers.

The square's neo-classical design was proposed by John Nash in the 1820s. He unfortunately died before its completion, but his designs were adhered to and realised by his successor on the project, Charles Barry. Work began on the square in 1829, and developments continued throughout the nineteenth century.

The square was built in honour of Admiral Lord Nelson, and named Trafalgar after the Spanish Cape where he historically lost his life claiming victory for his country against Napoleon and the French and Spanish fleets. Construction began on the column on which Nelson stands in 1840, and took three years to complete. The top of the column is decorated with Acanthus leaves, cast from British cannons, and four bronze relief panels, portraying Admiral Nelson's four greatest victories, are displayed on the base of the column. These relief panels were cast from armaments seized from the French. At the four corners of the base sit the guardian-like Lions, unveiled in 1868. These are made of bronze, and were designed by Edwin Landseer. Folklore states that should the bell of Big Ben ever sound thirteen times, these four lions will rise up and rampage through the streets of London.

The statue of Nelson itself is 5.4 m (18 ft) tall, although it appears much smaller when seen from the ground. Nelson's column is surrounded by statues of many other eminent and celebrated men. The Victorian major generals, Havelock and Napier, stand to either side of the column, and busts of notable military leaders front the North wall. The equestrian statue of George IV, which the King himself commissioned, stands in the north-east corner.

Trafalgar Square is encircled by imposing buildings. Its north side is occupied by the National Gallery, with the Church of St. Martin-in-the-Fields to the north-east. Canada House, designed by Sir Robert Smirke, who also created the British Museum, is west of the square. South Africa House stands to the east. The southern end is more open and commands views down to Whitehall, but is also the location of a statue of Charles I astride his steed, and the marked spot from which all distances to and from London are measured. South-west of the square is Admiralty Arch, beyond which The Mall leads down to Buckingham Palace.

A regular annual feature in Trafalgar Square since the mid-twentieth century is the enormous spruce tree which is sent to Britain as a Christmas gift from the people of Norway. It represents their gratitude for the part which Britain played in Norway's liberation during the Second World War. This huge illuminated Christmas tree is a fantastic sight which draws crowds of festive admirers.

Tyne Bridge

There are six bridges which cross the River Tyne, linking Newcastle to Gateshead, but the Tyne Bridge is undeniably the most recognisable. The opening of this bridge by King George V on October 10, 1928, was a grand occasion for the city of Newcastle. Children were awarded a day's holiday from school, and the congestion which resulted from traffic wishing to use the bridge in the days following its opening was unparalleled. The official title of the bridge is the George V Bridge, but it has come to be more commonly known by the name of the river which runs underneath it.

Dorman Long of Middlesborough was appointed to construct the bridge, and work began in 1925. The two halves of the body of the bridge, which stretched out from the opposite banks of the Tyne, finally connected over the river three years later in 1928. With the arch secured, work then began on the road deck. Lastly, the two large Cornish granite-faced towers were completed and the bridge was ready to be opened. A popular joke at the time of the bridge's completion was that the structure was highly unlikely to remain standing as it had been built on Sandhill on one side and on snowballs on the other. This referred to the furniture store, Snowballs, in Gateshead, which stood at the very end of the bridge.

The towers, although conforming externally to their original design, have never been finished in accordance with the plans for the internal structures. Originally, they were due to be storage areas on five storeys. The floors were never completed and the inside is now merely one large area used for storing equipment for the Sunday market. Passenger lifts were installed inside the towers, but these are no longer in use.

It is widely believed that the Sydney Harbour Bridge is modelled on the Tyne Bridge as they are indeed very similar in appearance and were manufactured at approximately the same time. This claim is, however, untrue. Although the Sydney Harbour Bridge was completed four years after the Tyne Bridge in 1932, plans for its construction had actually been confirmed nine months prior to the approval of the bridge in Newcastle. Until the completion of the Sydney Harbour Bridge, the Tyne Bridge could claim to be the largest single span bridge in the world but, when finished, its Australian counterpart was much larger. Both structures were, in fact, influenced by the Hell Gate Bridge in New York.

The Tyne Bridge cost £1,200,000 to complete, and its arch comprised of 3,500 tonnes of steel. The government provided funding for 60 percent of the construction costs. The bridge's phenomenal popularity was likely to have been due to the fact that it was the first toll-free bridge to be constructed in the area. Within years, other bridges had followed its example and also removed all crossing charges. When King George opened the bridge, he declared it to be a testament to the prominent position the North had held in the Industrial Revolution and in the manufacturing industry.

Over 60,000 vehicles now use the bridge on a daily basis. This amount of traffic was wearing down the road and walkways of the 1928 structure, and therefore in 1999 resurfacing and waterproofing work commenced, at a cost of £1,400,000. In 2000, the bridge was repainted in the original colour of 1928. Pressure has recently been relieved on the Tyne Bridge by the improved Redheugh Bridge and the construction of St. James's Boulevard.

Wells Cathedral

The attractive city of Wells in Somerset is one of the smallest cathedral cities in Britain. Taking its name from the three springs in the grounds of the old Bishop's Palace, Wells is a holy city, and it is dominated by its twelfth century cathedral. Wells boasts one of the best surviving examples of a full cathedral complex in Britain, built entirely in the Gothic style.

The first church on the site near the wells was built in 705, but it was not until the late twelfth century that work began on the present cathedral. Construction then continued in stages until 1508. Most of the cathedral dates back to the twelfth and thirteenth centuries. Among the features constructed during this period are the cathedral nave, with its elaborate foliage carvings, and the glorious west front, the pride of Wells Cathedral. The west front is an amazing sculpture gallery displaying an array of almost 400 figures, kings, saints, angels and biblical characters, the only surviving medieval example of its kind in Britain. Built between 1230 and 1250, but restored in 1986, the figures are all original except for the figure of Christ which was installed in the uppermost niche in 1985.

The cathedral's three towers were built in the fourteenth and fifteenth centuries, and the east end and Chapter House were almost completely rebuilt during this time. The strengthening arches, to which the interior of the cathedral owes its distinctive appearance, were installed where the nave and transepts meet. These arches were built to support the magnificent central tower which had begun to lean slightly westwards as a result of the weak foundations upon which it had been constructed.

High in the north transept is the cathedral clock which dates back to the end of the fourteenth century. The clock's dial is over 1.8 m (6 ft) across, and the earth is represented in the centre with two circles around it. The rotating sun around the earth denotes the hours, and the minutes are indicated by the star which rotates around the inner circle. The clock chimes every quarter-hour, but on the hour the figures of the knights on horseback above the dial engage in a jousting tournament until one of them is knocked from his horse. The clock is mentioned in the records of the cathedral as far back as 1392, and the original mechanism was in use until 1835 when it was replaced by a modern movement.

Inextricably linked to the Cathedral is the cathedral close, a collection of buildings, including the houses of the cathedral dignitaries, which are also remarkable for having remained intact over so many centuries. A row of lodgings constructed for the Vicars Choral lies to the north, a cobbled street of fourteenth century houses in which members of the cathedral choir still reside. The main road, The Liberty, marks the outermost boundary of the cathedral close, within which sanctuary was sought by refugees.

The octagonal Chapter House adjoins the cathedral on the north side. Dating from 1300, the Chapter House was the venue for the daily meetings of the cathedral canons, the seats of whom were built against the walls of the House. To the south of the cathedral are the cloister and the partly ruined Bishop's Palace, a private residence encircled by a moat and surrounded by beautiful gardens. It was in these grounds that the springs from which the city takes its name were located.

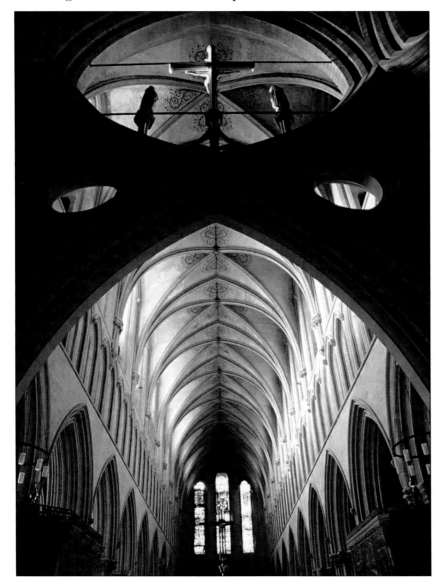

The Scissors Arch inside Wells Cathedral

Westminster Abbey

World-famous as the resting place of monarchs, and the venue for events and ceremonies of national importance, Westminster Abbey, officially The Collegiate Church of St. Peter, Westminster, is one of the most visited churches in the world. For over one thousand years, there has been a place of worship on the site, and since 1066, the coronation of every British sovereign, with the exception of the uncrowned Edward V and Edward VIII, has ceremoniously taken place here.

Little is known about the buildings which preceded Westminster Abbey on the site, although a church is believed to have been founded there by the King of the East Saxons who died in 616. The earliest confirmed foundations are those of an abbey constructed by St. Dunstan at the end of the tenth century. It was on the site of the abbey of Edward the Confessor that the present building was constructed. With its main focus on the church of St. Peter, Edward's abbey was built in the Norman style. Edward was buried in his new abbey at Westminster only a week after it had been consecrated. Within a year of Edward's death, both Harold and then William had been crowned at the Abbey.

William's coronation took place on December 25, 1066, and it set the standard for all future coronations, although they were no longer conducted in Latin after 1603.

The abbey's status as a 'Royal Peculiar', solely under the authority of the Crown and not within a diocese, was one of extreme privilege. It meant that the abbey was able to control its own finances and consequently amass a wealth which transformed it into one of the richest religious establishments in the country. A combination of factors contributed to the growing prosperity of the abbey. The royal patronage, the pilgrims who came from across the country to visit the tomb of Edward the Confessor and the labouring of the monks ensured that by the twelfth century the abbey was thriving.

With Westminster Abbey growing in stature, it drew even more attention from the monarchy who were soon conducting many of their affairs from it. Henry II moved the Royal Treasury to

The Coronation Chair

Westminster, and the Exchequer soon followed. The Crown was lavishly spending money on Westminster Abbey, and no-one more so than Henry III. The abbey which stands today is his gradual replacement of Edward the Confessor's abbey. He was determined to remodel the abbey on a much more elaborate scale, and spent notoriously excessive amounts of money on the project. Although Henry never saw this building finished, and some parts were not completed until the late fourteenth century, the French-Gothic style in which the construction had begun was adhered to in order to give the abbey a uniform and complete appearance. The west front, for example, appears to have been built during one period, but in fact the alterations and amendments to it spanned six centuries.

In the years and centuries following Henry's death, unfortunate times befell the abbey. Work continued but at a less enthusiastic pace, and circumstances arose which hindered the abbey's development. The Black Death saw the population of monks halved, and the Hundred Years War meant that royal funds were diverted instead towards the military. In 1540, the monastery was surrendered to dissolution, and its valuables pilfered. The Chapter House then became the property of the Crown, and the abbey became a cathedral. Queen Mary re-established a community of monks which Elizabeth then disbanded in her Royal Charter of 1560.

The building which stands today was finally completed in the eighteenth century, the last additions made by Sir Christopher Wren. Today the abbey continues to play an important role in the life of the nation. Sovereigns are still crowned here, and it is at the abbey that royal weddings and funerals are held. Eighteen monarchs are buried at the abbey, as are some of the country's greatest statesmen, politicians and notable subjects. The abbey also houses the tomb of the Unknown Soldier, the anonymous body which was brought back from the battlefields of World War I. Westminster Abbey is a monument to greatness and to the history of Britain itself.

White Cliffs of Dover

The image of the White Cliffs of Dover is an extremely powerful one. To the men who fought for Great Britain in or above foreign lands during times of war, the cliffs were their first sight of the south coast of England and symbolised their safe return home. Recorded forever in song, literature and art, the cliffs represent the nation's strength, and reassuringly welcome home returning travellers.

There will be joy and laughter and love ever after,
Tomorrow, just you wait and see
There'll be bluebirds over the white cliffs of Dover
Someday, when the world is free

The cliffs, formed by chalk deposits which are characteristic of the Cretaceous period, reach a height of 91 m (300 ft) in places. With only 30 km (18.6 miles) of water separating them from mainland Europe they offer views, on a clear day, which extend across the English Channel to the French coast. A million years ago, a chalk ridge ran right across from Dover to the Pas de Calais. Cut through by the Rhine to become the Channel River during the Ice Age, the gap has gradually been widened by wave action.

Due to Dover's proximity to the continent, it has been the focus for invasions since the Romans arrived on English shores in the first century BC. Although marking the shortest crossing point for enemies, the cliffs offered a view to the defending armies which stretched for miles out to sea. Julius Caesar, approaching with his legions by boat in 55 BC, is recorded to have seen the armed English forces lined up on top of the cliffs with weapons ready to hurl down onto the invaders. Caesar landed further along the coast in Deal.

The naturally strong defensive position bestowed upon Dover by the cliffs entailed the construction of many fortifications at this site throughout the centuries.

In contrast to the role that the cliffs have played as battlefield and defence station for the nation, they have also been the inspiration for some famous works of music and literature. In Vera Lynn's wartime song 'The White Cliffs of Dover', they symbolised hope and the faith in the promise of the future which led men and women to risk their lives in pursuit of a better life for generations to come.

Shakespeare Cliff, formerly known as Hay Cliff, was named after the great writer who based a scene from one of his most famous plays on the White Cliffs. In 'King Lear', the blinded Earl of Gloucester asks his son, Edgar, to lead him to the cliff edge, from where he intends to jump to his death:

EARL OF GLOUCESTER: *...Dost thou know Dover?*
EDGAR: *Ay, master.*
EARL OF GLOUCESTER: *There is a cliff whose high and bending head*
Looks fearfully in the confined deep:
Bring me but to the very brim of it,
And I'll repair the misery thou dost bear
With something rich about me: from that place
I shall no leading need.

The White Cliffs are preserved by the National Trust, and some areas have been designated as a Site of Special Scientific Interest. They are home to diverse wildlife and boast a huge geological and botanical importance.

Wimbledon

Rain frequently stops play during Wimbledon fortnight

For one entire fortnight, traditionally beginning in late June or early July, the focus of the sporting world is on the oldest and most prestigious of tennis tournaments, the Lawn Tennis Championships, played on the courts of Wimbledon. The centre court at Wimbledon is the most famous tennis arena in the world, and legendary victories and defeats have been recorded here. Tickets for this prestigious event have been known to cost up to £1,000.

The history of tennis at Wimbledon began in 1875, when the All-England Croquet Club, allocated an area of land on Worple Road for lawn tennis, a sport which was becoming gradually more popular than croquet due to the speed and physical demands of the game.

Just two years later in 1877, the very first Lawn Tennis Championship, an amateur event, was held by what had become the All-England Croquet and Tennis Club. It was an exclusively male event, and 22 men put themselves forward to compete in the Gentlemen's Singles. The Ladies' Singles competition was introduced just seven years later and thirteen women entered.

The popularity of tennis soared, and within 20 years Wimbledon had become an international event. By 1921, the tournament was drawing such large crowds that it was deemed necessary to move the event to an arena with a larger capacity for spectators. Thus it was moved to Church Road, where provision was made for 9,989 seated spectators and additional room allowed 3,600 supporters to stand. The courts of Church Road were planted with Cumberland grass and mowed to perfection. The Centre Court, the stage for the Championship matches, was believed to be one of the fastest in the world.

Crowd support for British players is strong

The new venue was opened by King George V, who with Queen Mary, became a regular visitor of the 1922 tournament. Prophetically, the opening match, which was supposed to begin at 2:45p.m., was delayed until 3:45p.m. due to bad weather.

A combination of factors affected the tournament in the mid-twentieth century. Air travel was becoming more readily available, therefore international players were able to fly to Britain to compete at Wimbledon, but the organisers were having to turn away professional players, ineligible to take part in the event which had been created as an amateur contest.

Initially unsuccessful in 1959, a vote to include professionals in the tournament was re-held in 1968 and this time the majority were in favour of opening the Championships up. From 1968 therefore, amateurs and professionals alike played against one another on the hallowed courts of Wimbledon.

For the 50 weeks of the year in which Wimbledon is not hosting the championships, access to the centre court is denied to all except the grounds staff. During the fortnight, the grounds staff maintain the courts by watering and rolling the turf, and trimming the grass to a height of 3.18 mm (0.125 in). In preparation for the tournament, the grass is 'bruised' a few days before the opening. To do this, two or three sets of doubles matches are played on the ground by the female members of the club. To symbolise the completion of the championships the Chairmen Four play doubles on the following Monday. The courts are then resown with new seeds for the next tournament.

Records have been made and broken at Wimbledon. In 1980, Bjorn Borg became the first player for a century to win the Gentlemen's Singles five times in succession, the record having been set by William Renshaw in the 1880s. Only two British players, Arthur Gore and Fred Perry, have won the competition since the first foreign player, Australian Norman Brookes, took the title in 1907. Players are remembered for more than their sporting victories. American John McEnroe's angry outbursts and temper-fuelled challenges to the umpire, alongside his three victories, have earned him a name in the annals of Wimbledon's history.

Winchester Cathedral

At the height of its greatness, the magnificent cathedral city of Winchester was unrivalled in eminence and second only to the city of London. A fine example of the quintessential ideal of the English heartland, Winchester, set against a backdrop of rolling hills and a beautiful river, is as historically noteworthy as it is picturesque. The city served as a capital for Alfred the Great and King Canute, and it was in Winchester that William the Conqueror's Domesday Book was written. As the centuries passed, Winchester retreated from the national limelight and returned to be the anonymous yet prosperous market centre from whence the once great city had arisen. A testament to Winchester's former greatness however, the city's 169 m (556 ft) long cathedral is the longest, and certainly one of the most famous, cathedrals in Britain.

The present cathedral was begun in 1079, but Winchester's first church on the site dates back to 648. This Saxon church was one of the largest in England, but nevertheless it failed to impress the Norman invaders who, in just over a decade after their invasion, had laid the foundations for a new building. With the new cathedral nearing completion in 1093, the orders were issued for the demolition of the old church. The location of the cathedral on ground prone to water retention posed serious problems for the cathedral in its first years of existence. Initial plans for towers had to be abandoned and in the early twelfth century the central tower completely caved in.

Work was carried out on the cathedral in the thirteenth century. The east end was enlarged to include a retrochoir, and the central choir and presbytery were rebuilt, as was the Norman nave in the mid-fourteenth century. With the exception of damage incurred during the period of the dissolution of the monasteries and subsequently the Civil War,

William the Conqueror's Domesday Book was collated and held at Winchester

the cathedral has survived remarkably intact throughout the centuries. The greatest loss to the cathedral resulted from Henry VIII's Commission for the Destruction of Shrines when the shrine of St. Swithin, whose relics had been transferred to the new cathedral following its consecration in 1093, was completely destroyed in 1538. The entrance to the Holy Hole is all that remains to be seen of the site of the Saint's shrine. The Holy Hole was a tunnel beneath the shrine of St. Swithin through which pilgrims would crawl.

The problem of flooding which had hampered the cathedral at the beginning of its existence continued throughout the centuries, but it was not until the turn of the twentieth century that it was decided that serious action needed to be taken. The waterlogged site was irreparably damaging the cathedral's foundations and before long it would be facing collapse. As it was impossible to drain the foundations, the only solution was to employ a deep-sea diver who could repack the beech-log foundations with cement. The man appointed with this task was William Walker, who worked underwater on the cathedral's foundations for five years between 1906 and 1911. The problem has not been entirely resolved, and the Crypt still floods regularly during the winter months.

The cathedral houses important monuments from all periods, as well as medieval wall paintings and nineteenth century stained glass. The cathedral's library contains perhaps the greatest of the treasures as therein is kept a tenth century copy of Bede's history, the meticulously and sumptuously decorated, and consequently unfinished, thirteenth century illuminated Bible and the first American Bible. Notable tombs in the cathedral are those of Izaak Walton and Jane Austen, and mortuary chests contain the bones of Saxon kings, including those of King Canute.

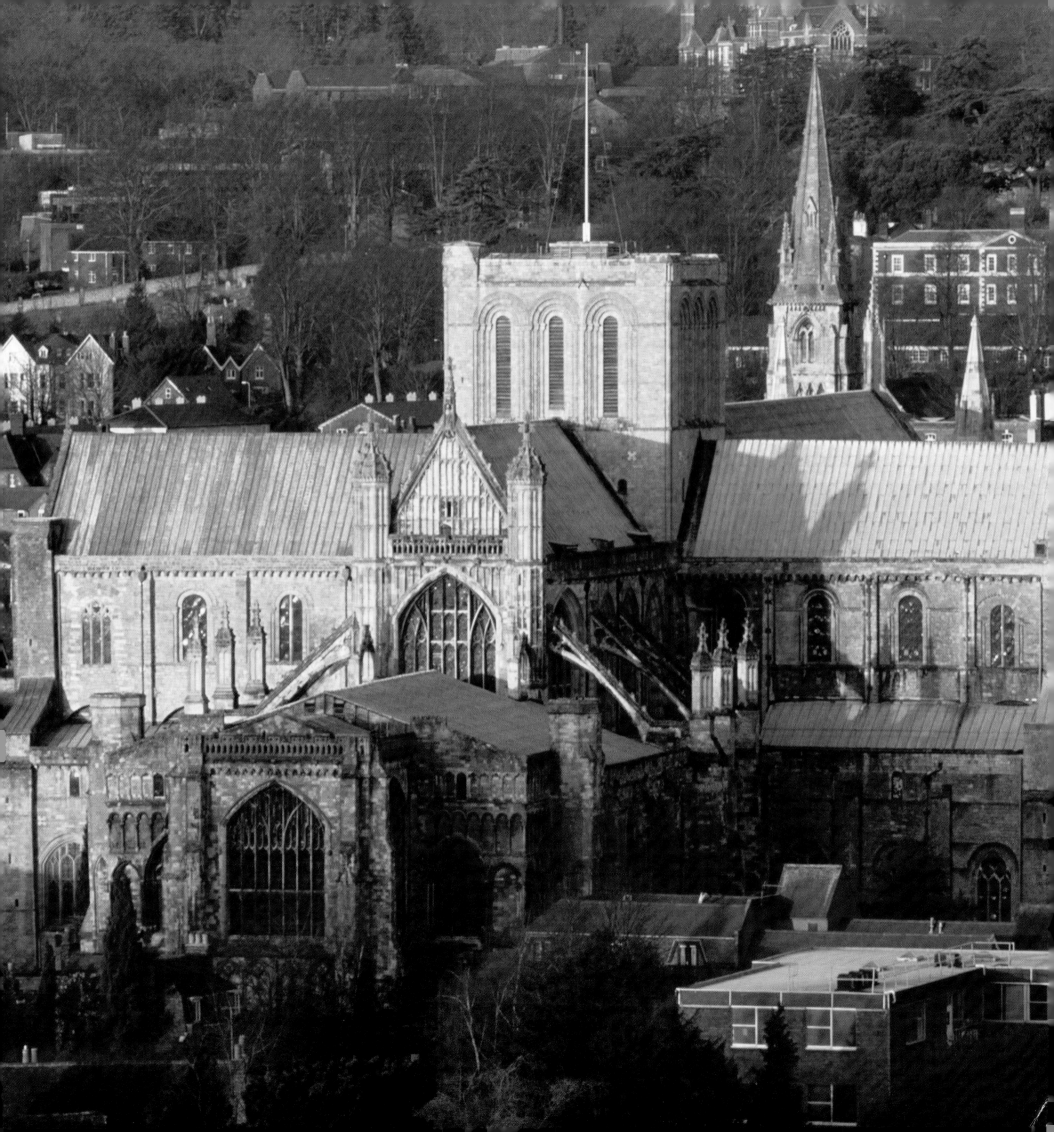

Windsor Castle

More than 900 years of British history are encapsulated in the royal fortress and residence of Windsor Castle, the construction of which was begun by William the Conqueror shortly after his invasion of England in the eleventh century. King William's castle was the simple motte and two baileys design on which the present castle is founded. Stone fortifications, the round tower, and the five circular towers of the curtain wall were added in the following two centuries, mainly on the orders of Henry II and Henry III, and further additions have been made by subsequent monarchs. Although William designed Windsor Castle as part of his defensive programme to guard London's approaches, so great was the castle's popularity that it was quickly transformed into a state residence and is now the longest continuously inhabited castle in the world.

The royal corgis out at Windsor Castle

Overlooking Windsor and the Thames, the castle is situated on chalk bluffs and covers an area of almost 13 acres, which bestows upon it the proud status of being the largest castle in England. Also included within its grounds are the magnificent St. George's Chapel and, as the castle still plays a large role in the official work of the Queen, the homes and workplaces of a large number of the Queen's staff.

St. George's Chapel is one of the finest examples of Gothic architecture in Britain. Begun by Edward IV in 1475, this rich and complex building is dedicated to the patron saint of the Order of the Garter, Britain's highest Order of Chivalry, which was founded by Edward III. The garter stalls are ornately decorated with the heraldry of the garter knights, and plates list the men who have occupied the stalls as far back as the fourteenth century. Meetings of the knights of the Garter are attended by the Queen and the Prince of Wales. St. George's Chapel is the resting place of many monarchs, and the tombs of George V, Queen Mary, George VI and Edward IV are located within the chapel's walls. The beautiful Royal Vault, located in between the garter stalls is the burial place of George III, George IV and William IV. Another vault contains Henry VIII, Jane Seymour and Charles I, beheaded on the order of Lord Protector, Oliver Cromwell in 1649. Cromwell's Parliamentarians seized Windsor Castle during the English civil war and used it as a prison for over a decade until the restoration of the monarchy.

The state apartments play a pivotal role in the function of Windsor Castle in its capacity as official residence of the Queen. These formal, grandiose rooms are used on the occasion of official visits, state business and ceremonial traditions and also display museum-style exhibitions. They, like many other features of the castle, have been redesigned and expanded for both aesthetic and practical purposes. The lavishly painted ceilings were commissioned by Charles II in the seventeenth century, and refurbishments were continued in the early nineteenth century by George IV and William IV.

Over the course of one night however, much of the beauty and tradition which Windsor Castle had amassed during its previous nine centuries of existence was destroyed. On November 20, 1992, a fire broke out in the Private Chapel of the castle. Nine principal rooms, including St. George's Hall, and over 100 others, were damaged or destroyed in the blaze which took fifteen hours and more than 1,500,000 gallons of water to extinguish. The following five years witnessed the greatest restoration project to be undertaken in Britain in the twentieth century. The skilful and beautiful restoration was completed in 1997 and had cost £37,000,000. The reopening of Windsor Castle coincided with the fiftieth wedding anniversary of the Queen and Prince Philip for which a ball was held at the newly-restored castle.

The fire at Windsor Castle, November 20, 1992

York Minster

York Minster is located on a site at which prayer has been offered for over 1,000 years, and the cathedral receives more than 2,000,000 visitors, be they tourists or pilgrims, every year. The cathedral is the largest Gothic cathedral in northern Europe and it proudly towers over the city of York, the adopted capital of the North. The site of York Minster has been at the very core of the religious and political life of the nation since the Romans invaded in the first century, and the cathedral is now the seat of the Archbishop of York, preceded only in ecclesiastical importance by the Archbishop of Canterbury.

By 314 AD, York had its own bishop, but the first building to occupy the site of York Minster was believed to be the military headquarters constructed there by the Romans. When the mission of St. Augustine arrived in England at the end of the sixth century, it was instructed to establish governing Archbishoprics at London and York, the two former Roman capitals. Although the Archbishopric of London was never formed, that of York was successfully founded by St. Paulinus, and it is believed to be this small church which formed the basis of the grand cathedral which stands in its place today.

The site of this original church, a wooden chapel constructed for St. Paulinus's baptism of King Edwin in 627, is shown in the crypt of the present cathedral. Subsequent churches were built at the site, some incorporating the buildings which had preceded them, and some destined only to fall into disrepair or be actively destroyed. Some features of the Norman church, which was built towards the end of the eleventh century, are still visible in the foundations and crypt of York Minster.

In 1220, work commenced on the present cathedral and it continued over two and half centuries. The cathedral's design thus comprises a number of different architectural styles, ranging from the Early English style of the mid-thirteenth century to the perpendicular style of the late fifteenth century. Work was undertaken first on the North and South transepts, the North becoming renowned for its five beautiful lancet windows known as the 'Five Sisters'. The Central Tower was built at the same time,

although this survived less than two centuries, collapsing in 1407. The Chapter House, heart of the Minster and from where its daily business was conducted, was also built in the thirteenth century.

When, in 1472, the central tower which had fallen in 1407 had been rebuilt, York Minster was declared to be complete and was rededicated. This perfect state lasted only until the English Reformation during which the cathedral suffered heavy damages. Further destruction was caused by Edward VI who tore down the chantry chapels and altars, but the damage done during both these periods was far outweighed by that caused by Elizabeth I. On Elizabeth's orders, York Minster was completely stripped of its memorials, heraldry, stained-glass and tombs.

When York was besieged by Parliamentary forces during the Civil War, the cathedral was saved only by Cromwell's general, Thomas Fairfax, whose ancestors were from Yorkshire.

Having survived royal ransacking and the ravages of civil war, York Minster finally fell victim to fashion, when in 1730, Lord Burlington's design for a new marble floor necessitated the destruction of every remaining tomb in the nave and many of those in the transepts and choir. Some of the building was further damaged by fires during the Victorian period, but the twentieth century has seen much restorative and repair work undertaken on the cathedral.

York skyline with York Minster in the background

Index

Page numbers in **bold** refer to the main entries

Picture Acknowledgements

Where necessary, abbreviations are as follows:
t = top; b = bottom; c = centre; l = left; r = right

Aintree Racecourse p.13
Pierino Algieri, Algieri-Images, p.130t
Althorp, www.althorp.com p.15t & b
P. W. Batchelor, www.ozimages.com.au, p.122t,
Bath and North East Somerset Council, p.140
Bridgeman Art Library (www.bridgeman.co.uk) p.63
Ian Buss, www.arundel.org.uk, p.18b
Michael W. Cook, www.castles-abbeys.co.uk, p.25, 159
From a postcard published by: Nicholas Charlesworth Postcards.www.vaudeville-postcards.com, p.32r
Adrian Crofton, p.134
Dover District Council, pp.64, 181
Fishbourne Roman Palace/Sussex Archaeological Society pp.74, 75
Jarrold Publishing, p.95
Michael Leuty, p.54
Courtesy of www.lochaber.com, p.28 l,r
Akifumi Murata, www.gallery-muk.com, p.108l, 154l & r
Photography by Colin Palmer - www.buyimage.co.uk - contact 01279 757917, pp. 53, 69, 117, 137, 158t & b
Professional Sport, p.183
Barry Senior, p.72l
Phil Sheldon Golf Picture Library, pp.156l, 157
Peter Stubbs, www.edinphoto.org.uk, p.77
Courtesy of the artist, Graham Turner (www.studio88.co.uk), p.37
Courtesy of the Warne Archive, Reproduced by permission of Frederick Warne & Co, p.104r
Watermouth Cove Cottages, www.watermouthcove.co.uk, p.72r
Richard Welsby, www.richardwelsby.com, p.135
Robin Widdison, www.dur.ac.uk, p.66

Collections Picture Library
pp. 21, 29, 38, 39, 45, 47, 79, 96, 101, 131, 132, 133, 155, 173
Freefoto.Com, www.freefoto.com
pp. 10, 16l & r, 17, 19, 22, 26t, 27, 30b, 31, 33, 40, 41, 49, 50r,
51, 55, 56r, 57, 59, 60, 61, 67, 80l & r, 81, 84, 85, 102, 103,
105, 107, 111, 112, 113, 124, 125, 127, 130b, 138r, 141, 147, 148,
149, 151, 161, 163, 164r, 168r, 169, 172l & r, 174, 175, 188b, 189,
Getty Images, www.gettyimages.com
pp. 65, 71, 73, 89, 91, 97, 115, 116, 142, 166, 171, 179, 180, 185, 187
Mary Evans Picture Library, www.mepl.co.uk
pp. 8l, 18t, 24, 34r, 36c, 42, 44, 46, 52, 56l, 62, 76, 78, 88, 94t, 120, 122r, 138l,
Mirrorpix.Com, www.mirrorpix.com
pp. 8c, 9, 12t & b, 14t & b, 15r, 20, 23, 30t, 34l, 35, 43, 48t, 50l, 70, 82, 83, 90, 92t & b, 93,
94r, 98, 99, 100t & b, 104b, 106, 108r, 109, 110r, 114t & b, 121, 123,
126, 128t & b, 136t & b, 139, 143, 144, 145, 146, 150r, 152, 153, 156t,
160, 162, 170l & r, 176, 177, 178, 182t & b, 186t, 188t,

BACK COVER (main picture): Richard Welsby, www.richardwelsby.com